BREMERHAVEN
A MEMOIR OF GERMANY, 1945-1947

BRUCE HAYWOOD

For Mary, who has given me a second life

Bremerhaven

A Memoir of Germany,
1945-1947

ISBN-10: 0-557-60333-1

ISBN-13: 978-0-557-60333-6

Published by EditAndPublishYourBook.com in association with Lulu.com

Proprietor and Book Designer: Michael Wells Glueck

Email: MichaelTheAuthor@Yahoo.com

TABLE OF CONTENTS

PREFACE

Early in World War II, my mother read somewhere that soldiers became dispirited if mail call brought them no letter from home. She was determined that her only child would never suffer a lack of news from home, and so she wrote to me every day that I served in the British Army, her letters sometimes reaching me in groups of four or five. Determined as she was to keep me in close touch with home and the life of my little Yorkshire village, she told me of every event in the lives of my parents' extended families, and added every piece of village news she could come upon.

In turn, my mother expected from me a similarly regular and detailed report on my doings, and I soon fell into writing two or three letters a week, a habit I kept up after I was stationed in Germany for two years after the war. Merely thinking to give my parents entertaining reading, I wrote at length about the work I was doing with British and American intelligence, though never including anything that might offend a military censor.

My mother lived to be ninety-eight, leaving me to dispose of the few possessions in her little rented house. I was astonished to find, tucked away in a drawer with her underwear, every letter I had written to her and my father while I was in the service. Those from Germany have become the basis for this book.

CHAPTER ONE

92 Intelligence Team

"To the Americans?" one of my fellow sergeants exclaimed, his eyebrows raised. He was obviously more than a little surprised by what the Area Intelligence Officer had just told us. As were we all.

The war in Europe had ended but a few weeks before, and we in the room that afternoon, who had followed the victorious invaders by various routes into Germany, had wound up in a holding unit in a charming spa, Bad Salzuflen. It was there that 92 Intelligence Team had been cobbled together, its members being selected without their learning why they were being separated from their units. Now we were being told that ours was not to reason why, but to go and work with the Counter Intelligence Corps of the United States Army. And so, a couple of days later, we did -- but not before the Area Intelligence Officer gave us a final piece of advice. "The Yanks play hard," he said with a knowing smile, "but they also work hard. Don't ever underestimate them."

I wondered at once why I had been chosen for this hastily assembled team that was to be sent into a part of Germany occupied by the Americans. The team, whose other members I was still just getting to know, was composed of a lieutenant, a warrant officer, and six sergeants. Before the day was over, we would be joined by a male clerk/typist, who was not a member of the Intelligence Corps like the rest of us, and by a driver, a corporal from the Royal Armoured Corps. A combat veteran, he had driven tank transporters both in North Africa and the European theater, and he was not slow to let us know that he did not think at all highly of the lah-de-dah types he would now be serving. Clearly, he did not think us real soldiers, and he pointedly wore the black beret of his Corps as an emblem that would set him apart from the rest of us. For security reasons, we were not allowed to wear shoulder flashes or badges that marked us as Intelligence Corps, and we wore pretty much whatever modest insignia we liked.

As was the case in every British intelligence team I ever knew of, the members of the ninety-second were men with very different backgrounds and experience. I was the youngest member, but one other was just a year older. The rest ranged between 24 and 36, one of them a budding concert pianist, another a grizzled veteran of the North African campaigns, still another a man who had sold some sort of British product in Germany in the 1930s. The one most likely to fit the needs of an intelligence unit had studied German in university. And there was I, barely out of secondary school. What was I doing, going to the Yanks?

Did the British Army know of my burning interest in American jazz, I wondered, of my boyhood affection for Mark Twain and James Fenimore Cooper, or of my having been an eager reader of American comics? Had wartime censorship revealed that I had an American pen pal, a girl in Detroit called Grace Fleischer? Could that account for their having picked me? My mother had told me in a breathless letter that they had done a security check on me in my native village before I was admitted to the Intelligence Corps, but would that have included getting into my enthusiasms? I remembered suddenly the admissions officer at the University of Leeds accusing me of having an American accent when I was trying to cover my Yorkshire dialect sounds with what I thought was standard English. I *had* seen a lot of American movies by then and I *had* spent a lot of time listening to the American Armed Forces Network -- for the jazz, of course, certainly not to try to pick up an accent. "You'd better get rid of it," my interviewer had said sternly. I didn't know I had it.

What the investigators would have learned for sure was that I had enlisted in the army at eighteen, believing, as my headmaster had told me, that the schoolwork I had excelled in -- seven years of French classes, six years of German -- would certainly qualify me for army intelligence work of the kind he had done in the First World War. But I discovered only at the end of my six weeks of primary training that nobody under twenty-one was being taken into the Intelligence Corps. So, being a big healthy lad, I was sent off to do infantry training. In the time I spent in camps on the North Sea coast, I learned how to march long distances at speed carrying a Bren gun, and how to scale a cliff wearing full battle gear. Fortunately, I never had to use any of the skills I acquired then, such as how to kill a man with my bare hands. For fate intervened in the form of an announcement on the company notice board that soldiers with dance band experience were urgently needed.

Nearly the only form of entertainment for the hundreds of troops in that huge camp near Berwick-upon-Tweed was the dances several nights a week, where the music was provided by the band of my regiment, professional musicians all. The band was being sent on a tour of army camps for three weeks, and those in command, concerned for the morale of the camp, proposed to put a band together out of amateurs or semi-pros in the ranks. I put my name down as one who could double on piano and alto sax, grateful for the couple of years I had had playing in a band that performed a small repertoire of the fox-trots, waltzes, and tangos of the 1940s. It was enough for me to claim the "experience" the announcement referred to, and I was eagerly welcomed by the trumpet-playing sergeant who was to be our leader. There were only a dozen of us who answered the appeal, for in those days few Englishmen learned to play musical instruments. But we went to work with a will, and we soon sounded a little better than awful. I was taken out of training completely for the week of rehearsal and the three weeks of playing for dances. It was the easiest month of my life. At the end of it I returned to training with another platoon, but before I was done preparing to invade Fortress Europe with the West Yorkshire Regiment, the need for German speakers had become so acute that the age limit was dropped and I was transferred.

Months of training followed at two intelligence schools, one at Wentworth Woodhouse in Yorkshire (a stately home commandeered like many another for the duration), the other at a former hotel in Derbyshire. I learned to ride a motorcycle, the basic vehicle for those of us who would work in the field, and to drive a three-quarter ton truck, just in case. We had classes on the organization of the German armed forces and their secret police; we were instructed in interrogation techniques, as well as in ways to deal with British Army officers who didn't wish to cooperate with us. But there was nothing in my official history that would have prepared me to serve in a unit attached to the Americans.

Perhaps there was no understandable reason for any of us being chosen, we concluded collectively over the next few hours. Like all soldiers, we were used to the inscrutable ways of those in charge.

On a rainy summer day, our newly formed team traveled slowly across a tortured landscape, over roads that suddenly diverted to avoid bridges blown by the retreating Germans. The warrant officer drove a small Austin utility vehicle with the lieutenant and three of us and our kits aboard. The others rode with their gear and four motorcycles in a Bedford three-quarter ton truck that roared and labored behind us. Along the way we stopped and drank hot tea from thermoses and ate the last awful British Army food any of us would see for a long time. Ever since the Americans had landed in Britain, all of us had become familiar with the gossip about the lavish rations they were fed. So we had high hopes that better things were before us.

Thus we came to Bremen. It was several weeks before my twentieth birthday.

CHAPTER TWO

The Bremen Enclave

The soon-to-be victorious Allies had decided at their Yalta Conference in February, 1945 that their forces would have to occupy Germany for a very long time to come. For the fear that consumed them and that hung over all of Europe, even as German armies were in retreat, was that an unoccupied Germany would rise from the ashes of defeat and bring on a third world war. (The Germans were, of course, uniformly blamed for the first two.) So, once the fighting was done, it was agreed, Germany would be divided into four "Zones of Occupation." Each of the Allies undertook to maintain a significant armed presence in its Zone for the foreseeable future.

The French established themselves in a small territory along a stretch of the Rhine River, their natural boundary with Germany. The British settled in the North German Plain, the Luther-land contiguous to the North Sea that divides Britain from the European Continent. The Russians had already overrun large eastern provinces and they quickly set about creating Communist East Germany. (It would be only months before Winston Churchill would speak at Westminster College in Missouri of an "iron curtain" that was coming down to divide all of Europe between free and slave. He was denounced for this by the *Times* of London and other publications, even as he had been denounced in the 1930s for warning of Hitler's intentions.) Ominously, as it turned out, the Russian Zone embraced Berlin, Germany's political and emotional capital, a city that the four powers were to administer jointly. But it was not long before the Soviets began their lasting efforts to get the other three out. Just as ominously for many Europeans, the Zone's border extended so far west at some points that Russian tanks could have rolled into downtown Hamburg, Europe's largest port, in about twenty minutes. The Americans won the scenic prize at least, for their part was South Germany with its Bavarian Alpine region, the traditionally Catholic part of the country. But that left them without a supply port in Europe, unless they were to go on using French or Dutch ports. And that they were loath to do. They needed to control a North Sea port with a sure railroad connection to their Zone, if they were to be certain of an uninterrupted flow of supplies.

So, immediately after the war's end, the Bremen Enclave came into being. American forces swiftly moved in to take over territory that the British and Canadians had overrun. The Area Intelligence Officer described the Enclave to us as "an American island in a British sea." It was a narrow strip of land some forty miles long on either side of the Weser, the river of the Pied Piper of Hamelin. The Americans, he explained to us, had authority over both Bremen, a major city some forty, continuously dredged miles up-stream, and Bremerhaven, the deep-water port at the river's mouth. In those cities, American Military Government would hold sway, while British Military Government would rule over the rural counties of the Enclave. That division of authority dictated a need for a British intelligence agency to work within Region IX of the Counter Intelligence Corps of the United States Army. That was why 92 Intelligence Team was created.

We were given little information about the CIC and its workings, beyond the intriguing fact that its personnel were called special agents and wore no rank insignia whatsoever. That enabled them to do business on an equal footing with commissioned officers, even though they might be mere corporals. One could not, the Area Intelligence Officer emphasized, tell anything about a special agent from his appearance, and it was well to treat all of them as though they were, in fact, commissioned. How superior that was to the practice of our own service, which kept us all wearing rank insignia, the great majority in the Intelligence Corps being non-commissioned officers. Once with the Americans, we could not, in fact, distinguish CIC agents from the civilian employees of the U.S. Military

Government, whose numbers quickly grew, for they alike wore brass "U.S." letters on their caps, collars, and lapels., but no other decoration. (We took the Area Intelligence Officer's advice and refrained from calling them Yanks, whatever their status.)

Our little convoy wound its way through the heavily damaged outskirts of Bremen and to the address our lieutenant had been given. That proved to be a very large, stately house that had evidently suffered no bomb damage, while its nearest neighbors were burned-out shells. There was a large parking area behind the house where a couple of olive-drab jeeps were sitting, with black-lettered "CIC IX" on their white bumpers. That told us we had come to the right place.

It was a German civilian, faultlessly dressed in a dark suit and sporting a silver tie, who opened the door to us. "Blimey," the irreverent Armoured Corps driver muttered, "a butler!" The German welcomed us in heavily accented English and explained that he had been instructed to show us to our rooms and to tell us that the commanding officer would soon appear to welcome us officially. The quiet of the house suggested that the Americans were elsewhere at their tasks.

The house -- formerly the residence of a Nazi big-wig, we learned later -- was a splendid piece of domestic architecture. As we moved in from the lobby, we found ourselves in a long, wood-paneled hall, so large that it readily accommodated a grand piano at its far end. My fingers itched to try it. To our right, we could see overstuffed chairs and sofas in a huge living room, and beyond that, to the right of the piano, a room with a ping-pong table.

The "butler" led us to a six-foot wide, carpeted stairway at the center of the left-hand wall, and, as we moved to follow him to the upper floor, we could see several white-clothed tables in a large dining room to our right, beyond which were French doors overlooking a stone terrace. We smiled at one another in happy anticipation of the meals we knew would be served there.

Our guide distributed us among impressively large bedrooms that were already partially occupied by Americans. I was put in a room where one bed of the three was available. I unpacked my duffel bag and then checked the bathroom, a marvel of gleaming tile and polished brass. There was an enormous bathtub and, next to the toilet, a bidet -- the first I had ever seen. The counter-top beneath a ten-foot long mirror held two washbasins. I could easily believe that the King of England himself had no better bathroom. We seemed to have found our way to wonderland.

The team's warrant officer, our office manager, stuck his head in the bedroom door to urge me to join the others downstairs, where we were to meet in the dining room with the agent in charge. As we descended those impressive stairs, my spruced-up colleagues exulted over the luxurious quarters in which we found ourselves. A couple of them had grumbled a little when we were told that we were going to be with the Americans, evincing the kind of contempt for the Yanks that many English servicemen affected, but now there was pleasure on every face. We grouped ourselves around the largest of the tables in the dining room and rose when the CIC unit's commanding officer entered the room. He was a strikingly handsome man; the name he gave in introducing himself confirmed my guess that he was of Spanish descent. He was a Californian, he said, and had been in the CIC since soon after Pearl Harbor. He had served in North Africa and Italy before being assigned to his new command. Our lieutenant introduced the members of his team, identifying four of us as German speakers. That seemed to cheer the agent in charge, who acknowledged that he was like most of his agents in knowing no German. He told us that there would be three meals a day: breakfast from seven to eight, lunch at noon, dinner at six. His brief stay in England before D-Day had obviously acquainted him with the country's customs, for he smilingly added, "Sorry, no afternoon tea."

Our first dinner set the tone for the splendid dining we were to enjoy with the Americans. The table settings, with sparkling white linen and heavy silver, would have suited a first-class London restaurant. We Brits exchanged raised eyebrows and smiles across the table as we were offered platters of veal chops and fried potatoes. There was rich ice cream for dessert. After years of rationing and meager British Army meals, we were overwhelmed. (I gained about twenty pounds in the two years I spent in the Enclave, as my lanky frame filled out.) We were waited on by German and Russian girls who had been picked for the job, in part, because they knew no English. In any case, the CO had emphasized, there was to be no talk at the table of any confidential matters. No alcohol at meals either.

Americans and Brits were soon comfortable with one another. We happily shared bed- and bathrooms, and we were quick to find conversational partners. The Americans were generous in offering cigarettes after dessert and polite in declining the Woodbines and Players a couple of our men were able to produce. Once bitten, I imagine. I found them eager to learn about the Intelligence Corps and the British way of doing things. They were loud in their admiration of the Londoners who had toughed out the Blitz, something that had evidently been widely reported in the States. They were the happy, big-hearted, youthful guys I had learned to know in movies, and I was delighted to be with them. But to my dismay I soon found out that there was not one among them who shared my passion for their country's jazz. There were some who liked the big swing bands -- Benny Goodman, Tommy Dorsey,

Glen Miller -- the music I liked to think I had "outgrown," just as others liked the bands that played pop tunes, the ones beneath my snob contempt. But Duke Ellington, Art Tatum, Louis Armstrong were at best only names to them. A great disappointment.

Our lieutenant instructed us to remove our stripes from our sleeves; in Rome we would do as the Romans did and go rankless. And we were to sew on our left shoulders the colorful U.S. patch that identified the Americans of the European Theater of Operations, which we, too, quickly came to call the ETO. The patch would tell the MPs and everybody else that we were legitimately in the Enclave. On the couple of occasions that I went on leave to England in later months, that patch drew a lot of curious looks from other English soldiers.

Next day the agent in charge gave us a brief acclimation talk at the unit's headquarters in the *Haus des Reichs*, a handsome and unscathed piece of modern architecture that had been the headquarters of the Nazi government for the region. What I remember most about that building, where our team would also be headquartered, was its elevator system. Instead of the familiar cages running in shafts, the Germans had devised an always moving, endless belt with platforms, attached at roughly seven-foot intervals, that were just large enough for one person. The belt ran so slowly that it was child's play to get on and off. Our first ride on one brought grudging words of admiration for German inventiveness from our most senior member. It was a strange experience to rise slowly and to see the feet of those at the next level waiting to get on. I have never seen another such system, and I remain intrigued by the memory of that one.

After just a day or two of settling in and getting used to the others' idiom -- easier for us than for the Americans -- our team was divided into three parts. The lieutenant and the warrant officer would be at the Bremen headquarters, together with the clerk and three sergeants. The driver would, of course, remain there too. (The agent in charge drove his own jeep, I must point out: different countries, different mores.) One sergeant was assigned to a subregion in Brake, a small town about halfway down the Weser's south bank, the place where I would one day spend my honeymoon. And another sergeant, John Garrett, and I were to go to Bremerhaven.

I wasn't at all sure what we would be doing there.

CHAPTER THREE

Mission

I had never heard a member of the Intelligence Corps describe its work as a "mission," a term the agent in charge used on several occasions in talking to us about the CIC. He had defined his organization's task simply: it was the CIC's mission to secure the American armed forces and installations against any attacks from a German insurgency. I knew that our purpose in the Occupation was to do the same for the British forces. Our practices, too, it turned out, were altogether like the Americans' on a day-to-day operational basis.

But nobody, including the agent in charge that afternoon, talked of a larger purpose. His focus, like everybody else's at the time, was on the immediate moment and the problems we might have in our day-to-day dealings with the Germans. But I found myself wondering, as I thought later about his using the unfamiliar word, whether there was a "mission" beyond the immediate moment. Just what were we doing in Germany, beyond making sure that there was no uprising against the Occupation, no sabotage of our installations, no undermining of our efforts to pacify the country?

On that question there was, from the very beginning, considerable disagreement, both among the Americans and the British.

Let me acknowledge at once that, in my early weeks in Germany, I was on the side of those who believed we were there to punish the Germans for their sins. That was not the result of my careful weighing of possibilities; I didn't think there was another. I had been a child of wartime propaganda that had portrayed Germans as Huns, Vandals, barbarians, a people so committed to evil that, as Winston Churchill had so inspiringly taught us, we should willingly sacrifice everything to defeat them.

I had grown up in a family that never had a good word to say about Germany. Ironically, my father's favorite musical composition by far was Handel's *Messiah*, but the composer was always made English by the dropping of the *Umlaut* in his name and by his being referred to as the composer to the King of England. When my parents talked of Germans, it was when they spoke of those in our village who had been killed or wounded in World War I. Not many from our coal mining community had served, and all who did serve, like my father, were volunteers. So we knew them all, even as I knew the names recorded on the village war memorial of those who had died. As the threat of a Second World War grew during my school years, anti-German talk intensified, even while people dismissed the possibility of any German success. Then, after war came, the Germans roused us from our beds with their bombing raids on a city nine miles away. We spent nights in air raid shelters, our gas masks at our sides, angry at those who were robbing us of our sleep. I went into the neighboring town to see rubble-filled holes, all that was left of houses destroyed the night before by bombs -- German bombs dropped seemingly at random. I read of Jews being driven out of Germany by a hatred that went far beyond the casual anti-Semitism I knew in Yorkshire. I had heard of the calculated destruction of cities like Warsaw, Rotterdam, Coventry, and, of course, London. But, closest to home, the Germans had killed boys I was in school with, lads just a year or two older than I, including Jackie Cooper, my rugby-playing pal and a would-be teacher of Classics. He had enlisted in the Royal Navy, only to have his very first ship torpedoed. So there was plenty of reason for me to hate the Germans, and to wish to see them punished -- harshly. It would not be too much to say that I went into Germany believing that the only good German was a dead German.

I have to think it a more than remarkable turnabout that, after two years of serving in the Occupation, I left Germany wishing to become a professor of German, before that a student of things German, to wish to understand how the people of "the land of poets and thinkers," as Germany was known in the nineteenth century, could have become the "blond beasts" of the twentieth century.

I did know, to be sure, something of their language. I had taken German for six years in my preparatory school, but I had learned next to nothing of German history or of the wealth of German culture. I had been taught and had learned German as though, like Latin, it were a dead language. The stories and dramas selected for our study were "uncharacteristic," like Schiller's play *Wilhelm Tell* -- which celebrated a Swiss-German, not a "real" German, freedom fighter -- or Lessing's *Nathan der Weise*, a drama famous outside Germany for its portrayal of a Jew in a sympathetic light. Or we read the work of Swiss-German or Jewish-German writers: Gottfried Keller's sweet tales of rural life in (favorably neutral) Switzerland, and some of the softer-toned poems of Heinrich Heine, all of whose "Jewish" work had been condemned by the Nazis. I daresay that Mr. Morgan, my German teacher for most of my six years, might have feared being thought a Nazi sympathizer, had he given us any positive readings of "characteristic" German poetry or spoken to us of admirable elements in German culture. (My French teachers, on the other hand, could and did celebrate our ally in their classrooms and were applauded for it.)

I was by no means alone in my negative views of all things German. There were many in the United

States as well as in England who believed that Germany should be held captive forever. It was a prominent American who put forward the "Morgenthau Plan," a proposal that all German industry be dismantled, German factories razed, and the country turned into a land of peasant farmers. If such an idea seems today vengeful and cruel, we should not forget the fear and horror that at the time held so many in thrall and made them willing to entertain such drastic solutions.

But there was another side, a different conviction, the view of those who were able to think for the longer term. They could envision a Germany cleansed of Nazi madness, a Germany of democratic institutions, a Germany true to the heritage of its celebrated poets and thinkers. Johann Wolfgang Goethe, Germany's greatest poet, had given in his *Faust*, the greatest literary work of the nineteenth century, a vision of a free people living in a free land. I had known virtually nothing about Goethe, but others knew him and were persuaded that his spirit could once again inspire his countrymen. Germany's greatest musician of the nineteenth century, Ludwig van Beethoven, had similarly celebrated freedom in the finest of his compositions, as had many others whose names were known beyond Germany's borders. Happily, the tradition those visionaries represented had survived Nazism, and there were leaders in America and Britain who believed that a spirit of optimism and altruism could be resurrected in a new, democratic society. The world knows by now, of course, that that enlightened view won out, and that a reunited Germany today is a vigorous, healthy democracy, although not without its neo-Nazis.

Every American can be proud of the Marshall Plan, which in the crucial years after Germany's defeat sent billions of dollars to rebuild that country, even as they can be proud of those who would not let the Russians push the Allies out of Berlin or starve the Berliners into submission. Today, Germany is in more than one way America's godchild.

Naive and untutored as I was in the summer of 1945, I could not have foreseen any of this. In the beginning I did what my superiors had decreed I should do. That kept me very busy.

CHAPTER FOUR

Bremerhaven

Sharing the cab of the Bedford truck with Corporal Pitt, who had loaded two motorbikes into its bed, Sergeant Garrett and I set out for the Bremerhaven Sub-Region, intending to arrive by lunchtime. That morning, I could not possibly have known that I would spend the rest of my army years in Bremerhaven, or that when the time came for me to leave I would be the sub-region's "oldest inhabitant." Unlike my American colleagues, who always seemed to have some idea as to when they would be "rotated," all I knew for sure at that point was that I was serving in the British Army "at His Majesty's pleasure." All else was uncertainty.

It was slow going to Bremerhaven, even slower than we had anticipated, for there were but one usable exit from Bremen and only one highway to Bremerhaven, a two-laner. For the *Autobahn* section that connected the two cities was closed off, so many of its bridges having been blown, either by our bombers or by the retreating Germans. Before we ever reached that highway, we were stopped three or four times at roadblocks, where white-helmeted military police viewed us suspiciously and demanded to see papers. They were obviously puzzled by the presence of a British vehicle in their territory. Then, once on the highway, there were lengthy diversions as we came to bridges that had been destroyed, even on that once minor road. Traffic was very heavy, nearly all of it consisting of jeeps and trucks of the U.S. Army. In nearly all of them were soldiers with carbines at the ready. We met convoys of vehicles on their way to Bremen or, very likely, beyond that to South Germany. German vehicles were rare, though we saw an occasional military-style Volkswagen with a spare wheel on its sloping hood and insignia that identified it as a German post office vehicle. Pitt commented that he had seen the burned-out hulks of such vehicles in the North African desert after the Allies defeated the Germans there. I would later hear of the Volkswagen "jeeps" having functioned equally well in the Russian snows.

The corporal, smoking one cigarette after another as he drove, kept up a running commentary on our travel, his invective divided about equally between the Americans in their vehicles and the Germans we saw riding bicycles precariously in the traffic or working on the farms we passed. Pitt did not love his fellow man, nor did he attempt to hide that fact. He treated Garrett and me condescendingly, but nonetheless as a desirable audience. That he was a decade older than the two of us more than canceled out our advantage in rank, he seemed to think, particularly since he had been allowed to keep the two stripes on his sleeve, together with his black beret, while we, our stripes removed, had the appearance of lowly privates. But Pitt, in all the months I knew him, never relinquished his conviction that we of the Intelligence Corps were not really soldiers. Once, hoping to rise in his estimation, I let him know that I had earned the infantry regiment insignia that I wore, but to no avail.

Finally, we found ourselves on the outskirts of Bremerhaven, where we were greeted by an appalling smell that I was later to learn came from the *Fischereihafen*, the fishing port. It was an odor that often held the city in thrall, a sensation I have never forgotten. The Germans had a considerable fleet of boats that fished the waters of the Weser's vast estuary; the source of the odor was the bulk of their catch being smoked. Thousands of Germans were virtually being kept alive by the Weser fishermen. The German population was existing on rations that kept them at a near-starvation level. Indeed, some authorities claimed that the daily food intake of Germans was below that needed to keep them alive. I never heard a German complain about the stench of the *Fischereihafen*, but every agent who joined our unit wrinkled his nose at it for the first few days he was with us.

I had seen bombed German cities before, Osnabrück my first, Bremen most recently, but I had not witnessed devastation of the kind I saw as we drove into Bremerhaven. There seemed to be but one road cleared, allowing traffic to crawl along in both directions like camel caravans crossing a lifeless desert. On both sides of us the remains of bombed buildings and rubble-filled streets stretched into the distance as far as I could see. Here and there a chimney stack survived, pointing upward like an accusing finger at the sky that had rained destruction on the city night after night. "The R.A.F. did a pretty good job here," Pitt sniffed, finding yet another opportunity to give vent to his feelings about the German enemy. At that point, I found no cause to disagree with him.

After what seemed an eternity we came out on the other side of the sea of ruins and found ourselves moving along more quickly, alongside us now grey factory buildings and the clutter of a working industrial community. Then there were houses and apartment buildings seemingly intact, and even more evidence of life in the form of fully leafed trees on either side of the road. We seemed to have crossed a line that divided death from life. We saw occasional German cars that had names already familiar to me: Mercedes, Audi, Wanderer, Opel, and, yes, Ford. Most often we saw examples of the tiny car with a two-stroke engine and a composition body that was called the DKW. The initials stood for "Deutscher

Klein Wagen" (German Small Car), but I learned
from a German that the letters were popularly said to
stand for "Das Krankenhaus wartet" (The hospital is
waiting). Now and then we saw a car that had been
equipped with the German answer to the gasoline
shortages of the last months of the war, a gas bag
mounted on the car's roof, a menace to the rest of the
traffic in a cross wind.

Now we were seeing a lot of cyclists, as well as
pedestrians in large numbers, some hauling firewood
in small carts, others optimistically armed with
empty shopping bags and waiting for overloaded
streetcars that lumbered along tracks in the middle of
the street we were following to the city center. The
Germans looked uniformly drab, war-weary, hungry,
downcast. Occasionally, one of them would stare at
the Bedford, noting the unfamiliar markings among
the American traffic, then look away with a
dismissive shrug. Nearly all the men seemed to be
carrying briefcases that seemed uniformly flat and
empty; I discovered later that the ever-ready
briefcase might carry a few cigarettes or a piece of
bread, if the owner had made a lucky strike
somewhere. The children we saw were bare-legged
and skinny, their faces pallid. It was hard to believe,
looking at them, that only in the last couple of years
of the war had the German civilian population
suffered any great privation. These children looked
starved and miserable. Now it was our turn to shrug.
We had won, and they had lost.

Corporal Pitt was uncertain about his bearings. He had been instructed to follow the streetcar tracks to a major intersection close to the CIC house, but when we reached the intersection he couldn't remember whether he had been told to turn left or right. "Watch for a big sign that says Bremerhaven," he insisted he had been advised, but the sign we had just seen, white letters on a green background, said "Wesermünde."

Bremerhaven, a city of one hundred fifty thousand people that is now part of the Bremen State, is located at the confluence of the Weser and Geeste rivers. Once called Wesermünde (Weser mouth), the name too of the county to the north, it is an amalgam of the communities known as Bremerhaven, Geestemünde, and Lehe. The dominant feature of the area is the vast estuary of the Weser that welcomes oceangoing vessels from the North Sea. During the war, it allowed U-boats to move undetected from their pens near Bremen into the open sea. Before the war, it had been home to Germany's twin prides, the trans-Atlantic liners *Bremen* and *Europa*, but now one of them lay in the estuary, a burned-out hulk, while the other was a prize in a French port.

The condition of the port's facilities indicated that the Allies had anticipated its postwar use and had avoided attacking it, saving their bombs instead for assaults on the civilian population. The port's security was always of prime concern to the CIC and to the American forces generally. We assumed that any insurgent attack by revived Nazi believers would be directed against the port, so we listened for any hint of civilian interest in the port and watched for trouble with the Communist-dominated unions of dock workers that soon came into being. The Occupation couldn't afford to have Bremerhaven put out of action.

My duties gave me little reason for being interested in the port, and yet I was often within its fences. For my favorite among the city's structures was a flag-bedecked hall on the river, built by the Nazis to be a yacht club for the privileged of their tribe. It had been recreated as an American club, its giant main room housing a host of small tables and chairs where one could sit and look out at the river and its steady flow of shipping. There was invariably a huge cloud of tobacco smoke rising into the dark beams of the vaulted ceiling. The Red Cross provided free coffee and doughnuts, but the real attraction for me was the large orchestra of middle-aged German musicians that played there on most evenings. When I was introduced to it by one of my new colleagues, I was delighted by my first encounter with a symphony orchestra and its richness of sound. Music as my family knew it had never given me access to such an experience. I listened to it attentively on many an evening, noting the unfamiliar names of composers and sinking deep into the enjoyment of what was for me a new form of music. I think of those evenings now as the beginning of my discovery of the richness of German culture.

CHAPTER FIVE

Welcome to the Sub-Region

S ergeant Garrett was two years my senior, and he had spent a year at Oxford University studying German before he joined the army. His German was fluent, and he used it now to rescue Corporal Pitt from his predicament. He hailed a German and asked directions. Once we were turned around, we quickly found our way to our destination. It was just after noon.

The house was not nearly so splendid as the Bremen mansion, but it was impressive enough. It sat in the *Bürgerpark*, the area that boasted the city's best dwellings, all of them seemingly unscathed except for a burned-out residence directly across the street that must have been a showplace in its time. The CIC house was three stories tall, looking rather like an English country inn. It was screened from the street by a low stone wall, with overgrown bushes beyond. A wooden gate gave access to the cement walk that led to the front door. Angled at the curb, with their front bumpers hanging over it, were half a dozen jeeps and, beyond them, a black Mercedes with a German license plate. On the jeeps' rear bumpers we could read the by now familiar "CIC

IX." Corporal Pitt parked the Bedford beside the jeeps and turned off the engine.

Fearing that we might be keeping the Americans from their lunch, we hastened through the gate, but the door was opened before we could reach it.

The man who greeted us was an American, no doubt about that, civilian though he at first appeared to be. He was wearing an expensive-looking suit and a flamboyant tie, his jacket hanging loose and revealing the butt of a revolver holstered under his left armpit. He was a burly man, five-ten or so, with large shoulders. His blond hair, lightly oiled, rippled back over his head. He gave off a faint scent of cologne.

I wondered at once what was the purpose of his dress, for certainly he could never have passed himself off as a German -- or even an Englishman. Seeing us, his face broke into a broad smile, and he stepped forward from the door in a welcome, saying, "Hi, I'm Dan Canfield, acting agent in charge. We sure are glad to have you guys joining us." We would get on with lunch, he said, and deal with our gear later.

He led us through the lobby, where carpeted stairs offered access to the two floors above, and into the long hall of what had formerly been one of the building's three apartments. Now the ground floor held living and dining rooms, as well as a den, with the kitchen beyond a closed door. There were a full bathroom immediately to our right and, beside it, Canfield told us, his room just beyond the kitchen. He filled the role of house manager in addition to working on any possible insurgency. The second floor provided bedrooms and a bathroom for other agents, each having his own room. The third floor was at that point without occupants. Only later did we learn that there was a second house where just two of the agents lived, the house to which Garrett and I were to be assigned. The unit was expecting a significant increase in the number of agents, so that both houses would soon be fully occupied, Canfield told us. (That "significant" number never materialized, and after a few months the second house was returned to its German owners.)

Tantalizing aromas told us that lunch was indeed waiting, and Canfield hastened to move us across a corner of the dining room through an arch into the living room, where a quintet of men sat. All were in uniform and in working guise, at that. They rose at our entry, and Canfield made introductions. One of them was a Hollander, an erstwhile "slave worker" who, like thousands from his country and other parts of Europe, had been forced into factory or farm work in Germany. He had attached himself to the sub-region as an interpreter and office hand. The Americans had dressed him like one of their own, and he lived and worked with us until his repatriation. The agent in charge, Canfield explained, was in Frankfurt for a couple of days of meetings, while yet another agent had gone off to Greece to hunt up cousins. I marveled that there was an army where blood could be thicker than red tape.

After we were seated, two young waitresses emerged from the kitchen, one a severe-looking blonde, the other a pretty brunette. Both were called Elizabeth, Canfield explained, adding that neither had any English. The Bremen rule against talking of cases or other confidential matters applied here too.

The furnishings of the Bremerhaven house could not begin to match the splendors of the Bremen mansion, but the food was even better! Garrett complimented Canfield on its quality, this producing a happy smile from the agent and an explanation. The CIC got Class A rations, the same as the general staff, but he had besides located a cook who had formerly served as a chef on German ocean liners. "Wait till you see his desserts," he said.

After we had worked our way through a more than filling lunch and settled into coffee, one of the agents opened a pack of Lucky Strikes and offered us a cigarette. Garrett and Pitt accepted, but I declined, saying, "Thank you. I don't smoke." "You'll be a rich man," the agent said. "Adolf can get you 500 German marks a carton, a hundred in our scrip." All of the Americans smoked, evidently eschewing the chance to sell on the black market.

Canfield puffed contentedly on a large cigar that went well with his burly frame and Hollywood look.

With lunch over, the agents were quick to take their leave, but Canfield urged us to sit a while and talk. He told us that things were pretty quiet in the area; they had no evidence of any threatening unrest. The Germans were utterly defeated, living "in holes in the ground" and desperately trying to find food. But he remained alert, he emphasized, for he was certain that, sooner or later, unreconstructed Nazis would try to strike out at the Occupation, and the CIC might well be a first target.

When Pitt, sated with rich food and Lucky Strikes, declared that he must soon return to Bremen, Canfield said that he would walk out with us. But as we came to the kitchen door, he rapped on it and opened it a crack, calling for the cook and the janitor to come out. He presented them to us, saying that Charlie, the middle-aged cook, knew English, having worked at a hotel in New York for a few years. Charlie promptly proved the point by welcoming us heartily in slightly accented American. Adolf, an elderly, defeated-looking man who knew no English, shuffled his feet, head bowed, but he raised his head and managed a smile when his name was uttered. I looked at him with interest, for this was the Adolf who traded in the black market, the Adolf who could make a non-smoker rich. There was no shaking of hands.

"Where's your transportation?" Canfield asked, bewildered, as he looked at the solitary Bedford. We showed him the motorbikes. "My God," he exclaimed, "you can't be riding around on those things in the winter. Doesn't your army give you jeeps?" We acknowledged ruefully that our army did not. "I'll get you one!" he said with emphasis. "Wait here a minute."

He was back in a flash with the two Germans we had just met, and he told Pitt that they would help him unload the bikes. As Charlie and Adolf walked the first one to the gate, the agent called, "Put them both in the basement." Turning to us, he added, "you won't be needing them." He was as good as his word, providing us with a jeep that very day. It was characteristic of the generosity with which we were treated by Americans, both by the CIC and by others.

"Put the gear in the back of my car," Canfield instructed Pitt, as he unlocked the trunk. It didn't surprise me that the Mercedes was his. The German pair removed the second bike. Then he invited Garrett and me to get into the car, saying he would take us to the other house. We waved farewell to Pitt, who lit up a Lucky as soon as he had the Bedford's engine running.

While Canfield was backing the Mercedes into the street, he said he would give us a quick look at the town before he took us to the house. As we were approaching the intersection where Pitt had gone astray, the agent slowed the car and pointed to a large, three-storied brick building on the northeast corner. "That's the police building," he said. "Our offices are on the second floor, and Public Safety has the third. The German police have the rest." (I was later to learn that the Gestapo had formerly occupied the second floor, an irony that escaped no German who was called to our offices.) "Your people blew the swastika off the roof," he added with satisfaction. A uniformed policeman with a spiked helmet of World War I vintage recognized the Mercedes and saluted. Canfield waved.

On the other side of the intersection, a bridge took us across the muddy Geeste River, and then Canfield turned right, entering another ruined area. A single street had been cleared, the Mercedes following its twists and turns through expanses of ruined buildings. On both sides were twisted girders, charred timbers, shapeless piles of brick. "The Krauts claim sixty per cent of the city was damaged," Canfield volunteered. A solitary church spire seemed to have survived more or less unscathed, though its clock faces were without hands. I felt a twinge of guilt. In one side street, a long line of men and women passed bricks from hand to hand, the bricks eventually reaching a cart. "Nazis," Canfield explained, "cleaning up the hard way." I would see many Germans doing such penance in the weeks ahead.

As we left the ruins, Canfield turned right onto *Hafenstrasse*, the seemingly undamaged main street, where burdened streetcars lumbered along central tracks in both directions and car and jeep traffic flowed. Driving slowly north, he pointed out places of interest to us. "Headquarters" a large, impressive building, featured a Stars and Stripes on a tall pole waving in front. It had, of course, been Nazi headquarters for the area. On the right, the PX, a treasure house to which Canfield promised us access with a card, even as he explained that we should not be entitled to use the Bremen commissary, where agents went to purchase officers' uniform items and such alcoholic beverages as they could find. (Later, friendly agents were willing to procure for me desirable items like shirts and loafers; I prized my American officer's greatcoat through my student years afterwards.)

The two movie theaters that nearly faced each other across the street led Canfield to explain that one was strictly for Americans, the other for Germans. Unlike the British, the Americans had a non-fraternization policy designed to keep Germans and Americans apart, though, Canfield acknowledged, it was "getting bent out of shape" after dark. He went on to say that the CIC was exempt from this regulation, as it was from some others. A particular exemption unpopular with MPs and others was there being no limit on the amount of gasoline agents could draw. Canfield told us that we would be given an "unlimited trip ticket" with the key that would unlock the chain on the steering wheel of our jeep. (Once again the American practice seemed to me more sensible than the British custom of removing the rotor from the distributor, thus making a vehicle inoperable.)

Among the dismal German shops we saw a GI library, with stacks of books visible through the storefront window, and then a trio of storefronts painted in bright red, with "LITTLE AMERICA" emblazoned across them in large black letters. "A place for the enlisted men," Canfield observed: "jukeboxes, pinball machines, that kind of place." I was impressed that the Americans had so quickly provided recreational facilities for their troops.

He braked suddenly, then hit the horn hard, saying "I hate those bastards!" in a loud voice, as a group of German sailors stepped off the curb to cross the street. They were talking and laughing among themselves, oblivious to the traffic. They were in full uniform, the only change from their wartime dress being that the swastikas had been removed from their caps.

"Your Royal Navy kept a couple of their units intact to sweep the mines in the North Sea," Canfield explained, his tone still angry. "They shouldn't have let them keep their uniforms, though. They're arrogant." The sailors had paid no heed to the blowing horn and took their time walking across to the streetcar stop. Canfield snorted.

He gave us a quick look at the port, pointing out the CIC's branch office there and telling us that two agents were assigned to the office, their job being to go out with the German pilots to check on the crew lists and manifests of ships coming into port.

Then, turning back through the field of ruins again, he took us to a second house, a much more modest building located on a side street just a block away from the police building. He escorted us to the second floor, but not before I had spotted a grand piano in the living room. Fantastic food, a jeep, a grand piano -- what more could I ask of my new world? Well. a maid to make my bed and do my laundry, a man to clean my shoes. Those were quickly forthcoming in the persons of a middle-aged German woman and an elderly former sailor who claimed his name was Joe.

Reminding us of the names of the two agents we would share the house with, Canfield showed us into the spacious room Garrett and I would share. I was disappointed, and felt for the first time that we were not being treated as well as the agents. But I should very shortly have the room to myself, for Garrett was soon recalled to Bremen and I became the sole representative of His Majesty's Government.

Canfield left us to our unpacking, giving us each a key to the house and telling us that a jeep would be waiting when we went to the house for dinner.

What a beginning!

CHAPTER SIX

Landkreis Wesermünde

M y primary responsibility was to provide intelligence coverage for the rural county, *Landkreis Wesermünde*, that extended north and east of Bremerhaven up the dike-rimmed North Sea coast nearly to Cuxhaven at the mouth of the River Elbe. It was a territory some twenty-five miles square, under the authority of a British Military Government unit that I was called upon occasionally to serve. I found its offices located on the north edge of Bremerhaven in a modest house that provided both office space and living quarters for its tiny staff: a retired colonel serving in a civilian capacity, a still active captain, and a factotum sergeant. They were assisted by just one German secretary. A shoe-string operation.

I knew the county first as a map on my office wall that displayed dots and circles for the numerous towns and villages. Blue lines marked the paved roads that criss-crossed it, while lines looking like a series of plus signs indicated the routes of the narrow-gauge railroad that linked some of the communities to Bremerhaven. I gazed at that map on my first day, seeing names like Bederkesa,

Hymendorf, Drangstedt, Weddewarden, Speckenbüttel. I wondered what Nazis might be lurking in those peculiar-sounding places, what breeding grounds they might be for insurgent activity. It was overwhelming. I couldn't think how I should cope with it all.

Additionally, I was to work in Bremerhaven itself on whatever cases British Intelligence gave me to pursue there or on matters the Americans might ask my help with. There was obviously going to be a considerable degree of ambiguity in my status and in the sphere of my activities. I recalled the Area Intelligence Officer saying, as he told us why we were being sent into the Enclave, "Intelligence work doesn't stop at lines on a map; there's a lot of overlap." There was going to be "overlap" too in my living with the Americans. The British would continue to pay me in the nearly worthless German marks they used for all purposes in their Zone, while the Americans housed me, fed me, entertained me, and -- at least initially -- provided transportation. My Methodist conscience told me that I needed to work hard to earn my keep, and more.

All across their Zones, the Americans and the British had faced the same problems in seeking to get a collapsed society running again. They dealt with them in the same way: they identified as best they could the man in the community thought to have been least friendly to the Nazis and made him mayor; they kept essential services going by retaining the people who had been running them; they left pastors, schoolteachers, physicians, and nurses at their work, expecting people like me to sort out later which among them were not politically reliable. Given the circumstances as the war was ending, there wasn't much else they could have done. On the whole, it worked out well.

The British Military Government had already created a functioning police force in the *Landkreis* by the time I arrived, and I came to count on it heavily. The newly installed mayors had set up town councils that were providing the inhabitants with their first real taste of active democracy. There was a surface order to many things. Farmers were at work in their fields. There were Holsteins grazing, there were chickens in the farmyards, and in every village there was a strong smell of pigs. Subsequent rumors told me of outlawed turkeys, notoriously heavy consumers of grain, being kept illegally in lofts, to be bartered to the Americans for cigarettes.

Before Garrett returned to Bremen, we ventured out in our jeep to get a sense of the countryside. It was flat as the proverbial pancake. Like much of Holland, a large part of this coastal area had been reclaimed from the North Sea. Dikes and windmills continued the work of keeping the ocean out, while ditches crossed the land, draining the fields. The soil was sandy and often devoid of plant life. Farms were small and poor. The farmhouses were like none I had ever seen in England, house and barn in one, with heavy, low roofs surmounting them. Piles of dung -- the visible measure of a farmer's wealth, one German told me -- were heaped close to the dwellings, presumably to ensure that nobody stole them. Like my native Yorkshire, it was a land that knew rain and fog, the sea always close. But it had its charms. The roads were rimmed with silver birches, closely spaced. The overarching sky seemed endless, and fleecy white clouds scudded across it on otherwise sunny days. There were copses here and there, homes to small deer that seemed abundant yet, surprisingly in view of the widespread hunger, were not hunted by the Germans. I quickly came to be comfortable with my county, eventually even to love it.

Fond as I was of the jeep at first, and impressed by its powerful engine, I quickly came to understand, especially when navigating the prevalent cobbled streets in the towns and villages, why one GI driver had painted "Kidney Killer" beneath his jeep's windshield. On cold rainy days, I recognized that the jeep wouldn't be much better than a motorbike when winter came. I began to think of emulating Canfield and getting myself a car, though he had warned me that finding one in good condition would be quite difficult.

But I was lucky. On an early visit to the British MilGov offices, I mentioned to the captain, with whom I always did business, that I really ought to have a German car "for my undercover work." He was ready to believe that the Germans in my territory would be less suspicious of an unfamiliar car in their communities than a jeep, and he quickly responded. "How interesting that you should ask about a car just now," he said. "The old man has just told me that we have to get rid of our six-cylinder Opel, because it's far too heavy on petrol for our meager allowance. That won't be a problem for you, though, being with the Yanks."

And so I came into possession of a fine, pre-war, four-door sedan, dark blue, with four synchromeshed forward gears. The sergeant turning it over to me said it had been mounted on blocks for much of the war and was in good condition. It was a joy to me for several months, particularly on Saturdays and Sundays when I went back and forth to Bremen. In my first few weeks in Bremerhaven I felt the need to be with my fellow Brits occasionally and to hear the King's English, but I soon became so comfortable with the Americans that I went to Bremen only once a month and then only to pick up my ration of Scotch and whatever other liquor I could get.

It seemed ironic to me that the Americans, who had so much else in abundance, were always short on alcohol, except for beer. In those days I was true to my Methodist upbringing and didn't drink, so I quickly found that I could have my very own currency exchange program. I paid in German marks for the Scotch, gin, brandy, champagne, and whatever else the British Army was willing to offer me, and then I sold it to my eager American colleagues for scrip usable at the PX and the commissary. It was the most successful form of commerce I had ever engaged in.

The backseat of my Opel carried as many as a dozen bottles on most trips, never enough to meet demand. I could easily have sold that many bottles of Scotch alone, but the British Army restricted that beverage to one bottle per month and then only to sergeants and above. (Rank hath its privileges.) In one respect, at least, I was an honest trader and a buddy: I didn't sell to the highest bidder. I held to what I had decided on my first trip: that I would sell for twice the price I paid, plus a fully disclosed delivery charge. This arrangement was always mutually satisfactory, and I was soon able to direct the Army paymaster to send all my pay to my mother. She banked it, of course, never knowing what it represented. Devout teetotaler that she was, it would have grieved her to know the source of my modest wealth.

But there came a time when my Opel, despite my loving care and the good American gas it was getting, needed a part to keep it running. None was available. The factories were not back in business after their years of building tanks and other armored vehicles. All stores of spare parts had been consumed before the war's end. I was out of luck, and my Opel had to be hauled away by the German police.

Three other cars were to serve me well over the next two years, until similarly unhappy fates overtook them. In my last few weeks, I was back in a jeep again, but this time a weather-proofed one. For an enterprising GI had found a German workshop that, provided with enough cigarettes and a few marks, could get the metal and wood to build a tight top on a jeep, one with doors and windows no less. Soon there were several of them in front of the CIC house, a couple even with electric windshield wipers, and one with the sort of European traffic signals that came out of the side like tiny, illuminated arms. In mine, a seat from a wrecked Mercedes replaced the passenger seat, but, for all of those added comforts, the jeep remained a kidney killer.

By then, though, my excursions into the *Landkreis* were few and far between; I had learned a better way of doing intelligence work than making sorties into the countryside.

CHAPTER SEVEN

Surprises

There were surprises every day of the Occupation. Some of them were at least very remarkable, others nearly unbelievable.

Soon after my arrival in Bremerhaven, I made my first visit to British MilGov, where I had an appointment to see the captain. It was with him that I was invariably to do business. The head of the unit, a former colonel in an infantry regiment, had been recalled to serve his country in a very different role. He seemed to have very little to do with the unit's day-to-day operations, but I often heard of his being away at their headquarters in Stade, as he was on my first visit. In due course, I made occasional courtesy calls on him in his upstairs office, where he made a point of showing off a German radio on which he could receive the BBC very clearly. That he was keeping in touch with "home" seemed to be a point of pride with him. I made a habit of giving him snapping salutes, civilian though he was, and it was obvious that he expected them. He always seemed to me no more than a figurehead, but he was a pleasant man, and I was sorry that he came to a sad end, as I shall later report.

On that first day, I was welcomed at the door by the sergeant, a friendly man a dozen years my senior, who at once let me know that he would welcome any American cigarettes I might be able to let him have. I let him know that I was a non-smoker, so that he would understand that I had none on my person. Before knocking on the captain's door, he introduced me to the secretary. She was a wan little woman with auburn hair, dressed in threadbare clothes and looking like nearly every starving, middle-aged German woman I had seen on the street. The sergeant identified her as *Frau* something or other. She welcomed me with a weak smile and in what seemed to me astonishingly good English. When it turned out that the captain was on the phone and not ready to receive me, I took an offered chair next to her desk, and, to my surprise, she promptly began a conversation.

Her "astonishingly good" English, with the accent of greater London, was in fact her mother tongue. She was very eager to talk to me, to tell me all about herself. She had married a German when she was a young woman, an exchange student who had boarded with her family. She had lived in Germany ever since. She had two sons, both still in school, but her husband had gone missing on the Russian front and, she said near tears, she had no clue as to his whereabouts. (Nor would she get one in the two years I knew her.) She talked of the difficult conditions under which she now lived, of the horrors of the bombing of Bremerhaven, and of her having lived peaceably with her German neighbors both before and during the war. Still a British subject, who might have asked for repatriation, she chose to remain "German" so as to be with her children and in the hope of her husband's return.

I felt vaguely uncomfortable with her, as though I ought not to trust her or to let her know what branch of the Army I represented. On later visits, I noticed that the sergeant continued to call her *Frau*, whether speaking of her or to her, as though he wanted to remind her that she had betrayed her country by marrying one of the enemy. But it may only have been that she seemed in every way, unless she were speaking English, to be German. I never found her to appear uncomfortable when being thus addressed. I still think of her as *Frau*, even though the captain, who considered her a great asset to the unit, invariably called her and referred to her as "Mrs." He always treated her with respect.

I must confess it had never occurred to me before I met this sad woman that I might find a British subject in the German population.

A second surprise for me was another woman with an English accent, this time a remarkable German woman. In time she would become my friend. She was in her middle thirties when I first met her, working as a secretary and interpreter in an office in the American headquarters building. As she rose from her desk to greet me, I was at once struck by both her beauty and her immaculate grooming. Her clothes looked expensive; her make-up was carefully applied; her skin tone was that of somebody who had never known hunger. She immediately expressed pleasure at seeing me in a British uniform, for, she would eventually tell me, she had a strong sense of kinship with the English. She was of south German stock, her father a wealthy landowner who had been able to send her to a Catholic boarding school in England for two years. Tears would come to her eyes when she talked of the nuns she was still in touch with there, and of the girls who had been her close friends. Then she had married a minor diplomat who had been assigned to London for a few years before the war. During that period she had polished her English to perfection and had feasted on London theaters and orchestras.

She would shake her head sadly over the enmity of Britain and Germany, the inability of the Germans and English to recognize that they needed to come together to fight against the Soviet Union. I knew of nobody more horrified than she was after seeing the concentration camp films all Germans were required to watch; I never detected a hint of anti-Semitism in her. She never made excuses for Hitler, but neither did she pretend that she or her husband had been actively anti-Nazi. They were "unpolitical," she always insisted. That word was a favorite adjective among Germans in 1945, their effort to explain away whatever role they had played in the Hitler years, their explanation for why there had never been any German resistance movement to speak of. But my Anglophile friend had obviously lived well during the Hitler years, as had most of those who adopted the same label. They thought of themselves as the "good" Germans.

I was so intrigued by Frau Ritter, as I shall call her, that I made a point of having a cup of coffee with her whenever I had to visit her boss. Later on, after the fraternization ban had been lifted, I would chat with her over a glass of wine in the officers' club, where she would be in the company of her boss, who was also her lover. She had sought employment with the Americans immediately at war's end, finding herself in Munich, a widow and an orphan of the war, her father's estate having fallen into Russian hands. Her remarkable bilingualism was a major asset, her good looks and breeding even more so. She quickly had an employer, a protector, a lover. I know that she had hoped that her first lover would divorce his wife and take her to America -- she had no hope that Germany could avoid being overrun by the Russians when the

Americans left – but, when he did not, she found another American. She always wore nylons; she always had enough cigarettes both to smoke -- elegantly -- and to barter; she was always well fed. She was a survivor, adapting to new circumstances with a determined smile.

In due course, Frau Ritter became one of my best informants, able to tell me exactly what we should expect of the German civilian population, what was particularly irritating to the Germans in the Occupation, what rumors were flying. Her one weakness was that she had no local history; she couldn't help me identify former Nazis. But she also became my teacher, introducing me to colloquial German idiom and local dialect forms, and, more importantly, talking to me about German history and culture. I have often regretted that I didn't keep in touch with her after I left Germany, even as I have often wondered whether she found a savior to bring her to America.

Far more remarkable than my discovering that an Englishwoman had lived in Germany through six years of war was my learning that two Jewish persons had somehow survived the war and were living in my territory. Everything I thought I had known until then had led me to believe that the Nazis' "final solution" had meant that every Jew in Germany -- man, woman, child -- had been caught in a Gestapo net and sent off to a concentration camp.

How great, then, was my surprise as I read of the two Jews, a man and a woman, seemingly unrelated and perhaps even unknown to each other. Their names and addresses were in a file left by some of the first British troops to enter Bremerhaven, members of an intelligence team that obtained its information from abandoned Gestapo files. I was quick to interview the two, the male first.

He was a cheerful little man, a horse trader whose family had been in that business for generations, he told me. Yes, he had been interrogated by the Gestapo, once before the war, once during the war. They had neither abused nor threatened him. He had always been on good terms with his neighbors and with the farmers he did business with. His sister had fled Germany after the *Kristallnacht* in 1936 signified the beginning of drastic measures against Jews, but he had stayed on, to be close to where his wife was buried. He had never had a sense that his life was in danger, and the Gestapo had shown no interest in arresting him. I wondered why. Oh, an obvious reason, he said. He reminded me that the German army was very heavily dependent on horses for its transport units, and the Gestapo knew him to be the most reliable supplier of draft horses in the region. He smiled grimly and said, "They would rather have live horses than another dead Jew."

When I asked him whether there was anything I might be able to do to help him, he waved me away. He had made contact with a Jewish chaplain when the Americans moved in, and plans were under way to send him to America to be with his sister. He would be pleased to go now. In parting, he administered a gentle rebuke by commenting that he had been seeing one of my colleagues down the hall on a regular basis, and he was sure I could have found information about him in a file. I never saw him again.

I deserved the rebuke. We were always supposed to check files before we took up an inquiry, and I should have known better. After he had left, I read the entry about him, finding there all he had told me. I marvel that he was so patient with me.

Accordingly, before I went to visit the woman, I checked to see what information the files held about her. There was nothing. Evidently nobody before me had had time to drive out into the country to interview her. So off I went. I thought of her, as I had thought of the horse trader, as a potential informant, perhaps particularly able to identify Nazis in the population.

She did not seem particularly pleased to see me. She was a robust woman in her fifties who had grown up in Cologne. There she had met her husband during the first war, where he, a native of

Wesermünde, had been stationed for a time. He was not Jewish, and she had never practiced religion, any more than did her family. Unable to have children of their own, she and her husband had adopted two boys, both of them lost on the Russian front. Her neighbors had never known that she was Jewish, and there was nothing about her physically to suggest that she was not of North German stock. She had taken on the accent of the region, and she felt thoroughly at home in the town where they lived. On three occasions, the Gestapo had summoned her to Bremerhaven, but they had shown no interest in her beyond that. She and her husband had always lived quietly and in harmony with their neighbors. She wanted nothing to do with the Occupation, nor would she spy on her neighbors. There were no really convinced Nazis in their community, she insisted. They were decent people. They were "good Germans," apolitical. That she said with emphasis. Her kind feelings toward them still makes me shake my head in wonder.

I was subsequently to hear from many an informant that Nazism had never really taken hold on the North German plain. Hitler and his people had generally ignored the region, preferring the southern part of the country where their real strength lay. The Bremen area was not a place of Nazi parades and Party gatherings. There were a few rabid types, to be sure, but people in the main had been indifferent to the government. Those who had taken on Party membership had done so to keep their jobs, or out of the belief that the Nazis really would introduce social welfare programs that would benefit them and the region. My experience led me to embrace that view.

CHAPTER EIGHT

Automatic Arrests

Uncertain as we might have been about our "mission," there was from the very beginning one sure guide to tell us how we should be spending our time. It was called the "Automatic Arrest List." The term, used by both the British and the Americans, identified those who were to be taken into custody as soon as they were located. We were charged with arresting them and sending them off to the Bremen detention center, where they would be questioned at length and sentenced to some term of imprisonment.

What the list contained, however, was not names, but ranks and titles. memberships and offices held. It included all high-ranking members of the National Socialist German Workers Party (the full name of Hitler's Nazi Party); all members of the notorious SS and Gestapo; officers in the Security Service; members of the SA (the Party's military wing) above the rank of sergeant; as well as lesser officials at various levels of the Hitler government. Then there were officers of associated Nazi organizations: the Hitler Youth, the League of German Girls, the teachers' group, among others.

For Hitler had brought under the umbrella of the Party virtually every organization in Germany, including the Boy Scouts and the Red Cross. It was a lengthy list.

We were also to interrogate and possibly to arrest all those who had been Party members before Hitler came to power in 1933, for it was thought that such people must have been among Hitler's strongest supporters and, therefore, potential leaders of an insurgency.

The point was to get these presumptive threats to the Occupation quickly behind barbed wire, where they could do no harm, and to impress all other Germans that we were serious in our intention of ridding Germany of all traces of Nazism.

We had been issued, besides, a very short list of actual names, identifying those charged with war crimes. These were, of course, the people everybody very much wished to be able to nab. There were only three names for our territory, and I was quickly able to establish from police records that two of them were dead. The third, a Gestapo man wanted by the Royal Air Force, was evidently alive, but in parts unknown.

So I gave my nearly undivided attention to working through the automatic arrest list, a task made relatively easy by the fact that the Gestapo and members of other file-keeping organizations, fleeing at war's end, had left their offices and their files pretty much intact. The Germans were meticulous record keepers, I'm grateful to confirm.

Before Garrett returned to Bremen we had made a couple of arrests together, but the arrest I recall with the greatest clarity was my first solo venture. Working alphabetically through a list of Party officials, I went out to pick up an *Ortsgruppenleiter,* the head official for a group of communities southeast of the city. Holstered pistol on my hip, I drove out in the jeep early one morning, having worked out my route before I left my office.

Arriving in the village that was my destination, I looked for a sign that would identify the police station. I knew the name of the policeman there from the list I had obtained from the helpful captain at British MilGov. This policeman had his office in the front room of his little house, and I found him sitting behind a desk, working on papers. He leapt to his feet and slammed his heels together as I entered the front door. A recently discharged soldier, I could tell, and no more than a year or two older than I. (The captain had told me that most of his police recruits were army veterans, and that all were politically clean.)

I told him that I needed to speak to the *Ortsgruppenleiter* and asked whether he knew the man. Indeed he did, he responded eagerly. The man farmed in the area and had been *Ortsgruppenleiter* for as long as the young officer could remember, "always" he thought. He volunteered that the man was a decent fellow, upright and fair in his dealings, much respected. He could take me to the farm; it was on the edge of the village.

I had expected that a Party official of that rank would have the best-looking farm in the area, but the farm to which the policeman, riding a bicycle, led me was a poor-looking place altogether. I had seen much better properties by now. Like virtually all the farmhouses in the area, this was house and cow barn in one.

A woman answered the policeman's knock. She was greatly alarmed when she looked past him, seeing me and the jeep. Her voice trembled as she asked what we wanted. She went off to fetch her husband from the barn.

I noticed at once that there was no smell of animals in the house, something I had begun to take for granted. I noted that the several photographs on the walls of the entry hall showed nobody in uniform. There were no left-over Party insignia to be seen on the jackets in the photographs.

The woman returned, her husband behind her, pulling on a jacket as he came. I asked simply whether he was the man I sought, and, when he nodded affirmatively, I told him that I had to take him in. The woman burst into tears and clung to her husband, but he put her aside and looked at me quizzically. I told him he should take his razor and things he would need for an overnight stay, but informed him of nothing else. He seemed to have expected something like my coming, and he seemed almost relieved. I stayed, uncomfortable, in the hall with the young policeman until the man returned.

As I put him in the jeep and turned to thank the policeman, I pulled out a pack of Luckies and offered him a cigarette. I had quickly fallen into the unthinking habit of paying with a cigarette for any services rendered. He declined stiffly, and I knew it had been a mistake to make the offer. The policeman obviously felt I had betrayed him.

We rode back to Bremerhaven in silence, the man bolt upright in his seat, staring ahead. When I questioned him in my office, getting the information I needed for the arrest report that would accompany him to Bremen, he was voluble, often lapsing into dialect in his eagerness. Like many another I questioned, he seemed anxious to tell everything, as though his recounting would enable him better to understand his years in the Party. (I had learned never to cut short a talker.) He told me that he had joined the Party early, impressed by its program of agricultural reform. His father and grandfather had farmed before him, working the thin soil and having difficulty making ends meet. He had done no more in office than to carry out the few administrative duties that came his way. He had not been politically active. It was a relief to him that the war was finally over.

The man was not at all what I had expected. I got no self-justifying statements from him, no accusations, no Nazi sloganeering. I could see no threat in him. I said as much under "Recommendations" at the end of the arrest report, where I quoted the policeman's testimony that the man was universally respected. But he was a locally prominent Party official and an "automatic," so I had no choice but to have a German policeman take him off to the jail. There he would be held until there was a shipment of prisoners to Bremen.

I looked at my watch. The one arrest, together with filling out the report, had consumed my entire morning. At this rate it would take me months to round up all those I was supposed to get behind bars. I felt utterly defeated.

Over the next many days I had the same experience repeatedly, as I worked down the list of *Ortsgruppenleiter*: a poor farm, a weeping wife, an unimpressive and harmless-looking arrestee. I could see no insurgency coming out of such people. And I could see very little progress for my efforts.

I was struck by the utter lack of energy and the absence of any hostility in these men. None of them had shown the slightest resistance, none had any thought of escape. They knew that the war was over and that their country had been utterly defeated. In more than one of them, I was sure I detected a sense of a guilt to be atoned.

Then I had an idea.

Given the utter passivity I was finding in my arrestees, it seemed wholly unnecessary for me to be going out into the country to find them. I could have them come to me. I could order the policemen in the area to tell them when and where to come. I could solve the problem of my time-use by eliminating a lot of driving.

I set up what our German secretary, Helga, called my assembly line, something she thought an American might have created, but not an Englishman. I calculated that I could get through eight interrogations on three mornings a week, write up the arrest reports in the afternoon, and thus send at least twenty-four arrestees a week down to Bremen. What happened to them after that was none of my concern.

I could at last see a light at the faraway end of the tunnel. For the first time since I had begun making arrests, I could imagine that I would eventually get to all the people on my lists. I would have Tuesdays and Thursdays to work on the cases sent up to me from Bremen, to read the denunciations that were coming in steadily -- and often anonymously -- from people in the county who thought we were mighty slow in getting the known Nazis behind barbed wire. I could even make a start on the crucial task of building an informant network. But first things first.

Helga took on the task of phoning the policemen a week ahead to set up the visits. I would hear her on the phone when I went to the main office to get a cup of coffee: *"Ja . . . Hohenzollenring Nummer eins . . . Ja, bitte."*

There were never any glitches. Not once over the many weeks did a German fail to appear. Not once did a man seem surprised that he was not permitted to leave and go home after my interrogation of him. Not one offered resistance when a policeman took him off to jail. I'm confident the word was out in the *Landkreis* that the day of reckoning had come.

Routine as they were, those mornings were never dull. I would reach the top of the stairs to the second floor and find eight pairs of eyes looking inquisitively at me, the men usually wearing the flat sailor's cap that was nearly standard in the area and what was likely their best suit. After wishing them *Guten Morgen*, I led them down the hall to a room where Helga had placed copies of *Life* and *The Saturday Evening Post*; at least they could look at the pictures and ads while they waited. I had a small pang of conscience when I realized that I could have told Helga to have them come at intervals throughout the morning, rather than have them all there at eight, but I was in the "punish the Germans" stage at that point, and I continued this pattern for several weeks.

I interviewed a broad range of types, ranging from the occasionally belligerent -- "What right do you have to arrest me?" -- to the usually apologetic -- "I believed what Hitler told us about the Versailles Treaty and England and France wanting to destroy Germany. I know better now." I saw the occasional face flushed with anger, men in tears, faces registering sorrowful acceptance of guilt in supporting a brutal, murderous regime.

Some of those I saw, no small number in fact, had joined the Party in order to keep their jobs, for after 1936 Party membership was mandatory for the white-collar professions. Among those were some who had then been elected by their peers to offices in, say, the teachers' organization, and they had taken the job reluctantly. But at the same time there were those who had been eager to hold office, whether for the local prestige it afforded or for the hope of advancement in their profession. I learned a lot about motives.

One morning, when I went to the waiting room to summon the next man, I was startled to find an SS sergeant, resplendent in full uniform, standing at the window with his back to me. Hearing me enter the room, he turned about, saluted, and clicked his heels together. He was immaculately turned out. Before I could put a question to him, he informed me of his name, rank, unit, and that he had been told to come in by the policeman in his village, where he had arrived just the day before. He said that he had discharge papers that were all in order. I took him to my office, leaving behind for the moment the next man on my schedule. This was a catch.

The SS man was a burly fellow, self-confident, arrogant. He had been stationed in Denmark for the final year of the war, he told me, and he had always had "very cordial relationships" with the civilian population. Above all, he wished me to know, he and his fellows in the SS had always been "correct" in their conduct. I had known that would be coming, for I had heard that same word from nearly every German soldier I had interrogated. It was as though they had been issued the word with their uniform, just in case they should ever be captured. His tone and his manner made it easy for me to believe he had been one of those SS men who, wearing jackboots, had strutted along the streets of Paris, Copenhagen, Amsterdam, Prague, ready to kick out of their way any native who crossed their path. I took a particular pleasure in writing up his arrest report and in shipping him off to jail.

But of all the many men I saw on those mornings, one stands out above the rest. For one thing, he was the only one who brought his wife with him.

I had anticipated his visit with some interest, for he was distinguished by his having joined the Party in 1928, five years before Hitler came to power, much earlier than anybody else I had seen. I was expecting the ultimate Nazi, an unrepentant quoter of *Mein Kampf*, a true Aryan representative of the "master race." He was none of these. Instead he was a pathetic figure, slight of build, frail, downcast. His wife matched him. I listened to their story.

In 1928, they were living in Berlin, where night after night armed squads of Communists fought in the streets with bands of rightists. The city was in chaos much of the time. Economic depression and years of staggering inflation had crippled the country, destroying any faith the people had had in the Weimar Republic. He was a common laborer, a man without sophistication or education. He and his fellows feared that Germany would fall to Communism as Russia had done. They could find no stability, no hope of being employed. He thought himself a good, loyal German and a devout Lutheran. He had served in the trenches during the first war and had become disillusioned in its aftermath. Thus he and his wife listened eagerly as the Nazis, in their first national election campaign, talked of restoring order, of creating jobs, of building a new Germany on the best heritage of the old. Hopeful, he joined the Party and paid his dues. He had never profited from his membership and had never held an office. But the years had given him and his wife plenty of reason to regret.

As I listened, I could hear echoes of familiar voices: those of my parents. I had grown up in a family of loyal subjects, devout Methodists, lovers of order, unsophisticated believers in their government's promises. Had my parents been Germans in 1928, they might well have responded to Hitler's appeal as this couple had.

I sent them home, giving the man a couple of cigarettes as they left my office. I was glad that I had no more interrogations that day.

CHAPTER NINE

German Helpers

What the CIC unit in Bremerhaven had in common with other American organizations that had dealings with Germans was its dependency on the natives to help it do its work. In the first months after the war's end, English-speaking Germans were much in demand to serve as interpreters and translators, but most obviously to work as secretaries. Until the arrival of the first WACs in 1946, the secretaries one encountered, even in sensitive offices like ours, were most likely to be German women. The former "slave worker" who knew some English as well as German, like the CIC's Hollander, was particularly valued.

It was a great surprise to me that so few of the CIC agents I met over my two years in the Bremen Enclave knew any German. When I first arrived in Bremerhaven, there were just three agents who had some command of the language, the one native speaker being a Jewish refugee from Austria who had fled to North America after the *Anschluss* in 1938. His English was as uncertain as the German spoken by his two colleagues, each of whom was quick to say that he spoke only "kitchen German."

Neither had had any formal instruction in the language, but both had acquired some speaking ability by growing up in households where grandparents and sometimes parents and others used German. The one spoke a South German dialect barely understandable in North Germany, though sufficiently so for his assignment at the port. The other simply used the German words he knew in sentences that were otherwise altogether American, but he usually made himself understood.

We would later have two other native speakers, again Jewish refugees. I found one, who had recently transferred to CIC from a signals unit, particularly interesting, partly because the agent in charge put him under my wing for his first few weeks. He was the son of a Viennese newspaper editor who was arrested the moment the Nazis took over the city in 1938. His father was never heard from again. The mother fled with her two sons, then little boys, and declared upon reaching New York that they would never use German again. My colleague, when I first knew him, had quite forgotten his German, insisting that he couldn't speak or understand the language. I was fascinated to witness his dredging it up from the depths of memory as he listened to me and the Germans I was interrogating. Day by day his response to it grew, and he began tentatively to speak. Then it was like a snowball rolling down a hill. I recall with particular clarity a day when I had reason to use the North German word for an orange,

Apfelsine, a word he had never heard, but it triggered his native word, *Orange* (pronounced in the French way). A little startled, he told me that he had been unaware that he knew it. Within a short time, he used German as though he had never missed a day of speaking it, and he became a first-rate agent.

But among the other thirty or so agents who passed through the sub-region in my time, their tours of duty sometimes lasting only a few months, there was not a single German speaker, and we never had more than two at any time. Thus there was always a need for native German interpreters. It was obviously somebody's good idea that having maids who knew no English would be better for preserving security. That same sense presumably gave us Helga, our one and only secretary in 1945, already in place when I arrived. She was a Bremerhaven native, in her late teens, and a slow typist, for she had to transcribe letter by letter from the handwritten originals the agents gave her. I soon learned that I could type my own letters in less time than it took me to proofread anything she did for me. But she knew how to keep files in order, and she made good coffee. Besides, she was a valuable informant on local happenings. She seemed to acquire very little English in the time she was with us; indeed she seemed to make no effort to learn it. She had to be dropped from our staff in early 1946, when the powers in Frankfurt decided that we and other units were risking security leaks by employing German secretaries. Our first WAC took her place, but she, alas, knew no German.

Also present on my arrival was a male interpreter who had an office across the hall from mine, a fortyish man who always knew more about what was going on in the unit than anybody else. Paul had once been close to becoming an American citizen, for he and his wife had emigrated to Detroit in the early 1930s. There was a job awaiting him with a kinsman whose firm installed radios in automobiles. "He always let me do the Cadillacs," Paul told me proudly at our first meeting, speaking fluent colloquial American as he told me of the ups and downs in his life. His wife had been as eager as he to settle into life in America, and they had taken out a mortgage. But soon after his father died in 1938, his mother had taken ill, and he returned to Germany, only to have the war break out before he was able to provide for his mother's comfort in her last days. He was trapped, he said bitterly. Now, with their home bombed late in the war, he and his family, including a daughter born after their return to Germany, were eking out an existence in a cellar. "You cannot imagine," he said wearily, "how difficult my life is now, or how good it was then." He seemed to come to life only when he reminisced about the years in Detroit. "We had good times then," he often told me.

I regularly had a cup of coffee with Paul, treating him to cigarettes on those occasions. He always put them away carefully for future trade. In return, he kept me abreast of the progress he and his family were making toward creating something like a life, a commentary in its way on what people in the country as a whole were experiencing.

George, the name pronounced as though it were French, came into our life many months after the war, by which time I was well settled into my work. He had been a detective, but had been expelled from the post-war police force because he had held a minor office in the Party. Nonetheless, he was recommended to us by the chief of police as a highly competent man whom he was reluctant to lose. Though George knew no English, we took him on as an investigator, after establishing that he had never held Nazi sympathies but had simply played the game that people like him had to play in order to hold a job and to avoid suspicion. He was in his early forties, a handsome Nordic type, highly intelligent, and very resourceful. He had extensive contacts in city offices, some of which proved invaluable in one case that he and I worked on together. We became close friends, and he would one day save my bacon, as I shall tell in a later chapter.

Ernst, too, came to us several months after my arrival, recommended by the British MilGov captain, who had wished to make him one of his policemen. A former infantryman, politically clean and robust, he would have brought very desirable assets to the job. But Ernst had teeth bad enough to make him fail the physical exam -- a consequence, he claimed, of the time he had served on the Russian front. He knew enough English to make him useful as an interpreter, and, because he lived in Bederkesa, a town on the eastern edge of my territory, he was valuable to me as an informant on the happenings in that part of the *Landkreis*. We spent a lot of time together, and I learned much from him about German ways. We always spoke German together, and he was one of those who wanted to believe that I must have been a child in that area. The fact was that my Yorkshire vowels and consonants were just like those of Bremen German, and, as I gained more and more fluency, I was able to pass as a native.

I used Ernst as a cover from time to time, since he was close to my age and resembled me physically. We might have been thought brothers. By the time he joined our staff, I had acquired a German suit, shirt, tie, and raincoat, in order to be a German among Germans when the need arose. I had Ernst join me when I went to sit in taverns to eavesdrop on conversations at nearby tables, his presence helping to ensure that I would not be scrutinized. I sometimes took him with me when I had a reason to go into the countryside, believing that I would be less conspicuous in his company.

But I was in full British uniform on the evening when he was especially helpful to me in dealing with what seemed at first like a potentially important and difficult case.

I regularly received copies of mail intercepts, and, less frequently, a copy of a telegram sent to somebody in my territory. It was such a telegram in early 1947 that alerted me to a seemingly clandestine meeting of businessmen from several parts of the British Zone. The censor imagined that this might be a meeting of Nazi sympathizers who, with Germany's economy just beginning to recover from the shocks of the war, might be coming together to create the foundation for a revived Nazi Party. The censor's suspicions had presumably been sharpened when he saw that the telegram told the recipient that he was to meet five men arriving on the narrow-gauge train at one of the villages in my territory. I didn't have much time.

I sent Ernst out on his motorcycle (fueled, like my car, by CIC), to find the location of the recipient's dwelling. My suspicions were heightened when he reported that the man lived in a small, remote house on the edge of a wood. He had seen no automobile on the property, but there was a phone line to the house.

The ruse I decided upon would, I hoped, give me opportunity to listen to the group's conversation over an extended period, without their suspecting I was there for that purpose. The house's remoteness became an advantage. The key to the success of this plan was my certainty that the problems with the German telephone system, still not wholly rebuilt, would guarantee a long wait for a call to go through.

I removed from my cap the Intelligence Corps badge we were now allowed to wear, substituting the West Yorkshire Regiment badge I had kept. I removed the American flash from the shoulder of my jacket, and I discarded for the occasion the American officer's raincoat that I habitually wore, donning my British greatcoat instead. (I had long ceased to wear a pistol.) I wanted nothing to suggest that I was stationed in the Enclave.

I gave Ernst careful instructions. We would leave the car at the road and approach the house on foot. Posing as my driver and interpreter, he would explain that I was traveling from Hamburg to Bremerhaven for a meeting, but that we were running very late because of detours and delays where bridges were being rebuilt. He was doing the talking because I spoke no German, and to reinforce that impression he would turn to me to translate whatever was said to him. He would explain that the wires to the house had told him that there was, unusually, a telephone. Might the officer use the phone to explain the delay in his arrival and to tell his whereabouts? I was reasonably certain that the telephone would be in the room where the meeting was taking place, and I could hope that, after a few moments, the meeting would go forward with us as silent witnesses.

The man who responded to our knock looked startled to see us. As Ernst made his pitch, he shot inquisitive looks at me from time to time, but showed no hostility. Indeed, he readily conducted us into the living room where five men rose to their feet, clumsily seeking to conceal the glasses of *Schnaps* they were consuming. But in the German fashion they bowed as their host gave Ernst their names and as he presented "Captain Sommers" to them. They were well-dressed and appeared prosperous, all in advanced middle age. Professional men, obviously. The host showed Ernst to the phone, warning of likely delay, and provided me with a chair. Ernst pulled from his wallet the piece of paper I had given him with my office phone number on it and gave it to the operator, then put the phone down to await a call we knew would never come.

I had prepared myself to show no understanding if one of the group should speak to me, and, sure enough, one of them did. I turned to Ernst and asked for a translation. That seemed to satisfy them, and they were soon talking as though we were not present. I shuffled occasionally and gave Ernst the word to try the operator again, but after half an hour I thought we would only create suspicion by staying longer. The phone's owner commiserated.

What I had been able to establish was that the men were bankers who were having a very private meeting so that their common interest would not come to light. Germany, they knew, would soon undergo a drastic reform of its currency, and they were seeking to agree on what they might do together to anticipate the inevitable dislocations. Later, I was able, with George's help, to identify the host as a Bremen banker who was now living full-time in what had once been his family's weekend retreat, his home in Bremen having been destroyed in the bombing. The place was certainly far from the madding crowd, a suitable place for a private meeting. There was no harm in these men, but there might have been.

My report brought me the only commendation I ever got from the Area Intelligence Officer, who described it as a model of imaginative initiative. Ernst was pleased when I showed him the letter. He had played his part perfectly.

CHAPTER TEN

Horror

Nothing I saw or heard in Germany matched the sheer horror of the concentration camp film I watched in the fall of 1945 at the German theater in Bremerhaven. The film was produced by an American Army unit at one of the more notorious camps, Buchenwald, immediately after its liberation.

To ensure that the German civilian population knew of the monstrous deeds committed in the name of their country, every German over sixteen was required to attend one of the many showings of the film that week. The proof of their attendance was to be getting their ration cards stamped by policemen stationed in the lobby. Newspaper and radio announcements stressed that a card without the stamp would be declared invalid, so we could be sure that people would attend and get their cards stamped. Whether they would then sit with their eyes and minds closed was another question.

Our superiors were, of course, interested to know how the Germans reacted to the film, so two of us were commissioned to watch the Germans watching the film. But when it came time to write my report, I could find no words adequate to express the loathing and disgust the film had inspired in me. I cannot now.

I had not viewed the film before the Germans did, and I had no real clue as to its content. So on the opening night I shared with the audience the shock and pain of its appalling scenes.

Before the film began, I had looked about the theater, noting the apprehension and anxiety visible on many faces, the stiffened jaws, the hands tight together. There was silence and suspense everywhere. Nobody knew for sure what was coming. But the fact of required attendance was enough to make them suspect that they were there to be instructed. They had, of course, remarked the presence of my American colleague and me, for we were in uniform.

As we stared at the blank screen, a recorded South German voice told the audience of the film's making and stated the number of minutes it would run. Then a moment of darkness was followed by gruesome scenes in black and white of men in tattered clothing standing helplessly beyond barbed wire fences. Impossible to know their ages. Some gazed at the camera with unseeing eyes and open mouths that showed toothless gums. They were living skeletons, skin stretched tight over bones, expressions blank. Some began to thrust their pitiful naked arms through the wire, as though reaching for help; others frowned, not certain that a trick wasn't being played on them. Others wept. It is impossible to imagine their misery. That no sound accompanied the pictures made the scenes even more eerie, like something from a grotesque silent movie.

The camera moved slowly into huts where sick, helpless men lay on bunks, some clutching rags, barely able to raise their heads. They were obviously near death. And beyond, as the camera passed through the huts into an open square, was the sickening sight of dead bodies, some naked, some still clad in tattered clothing. They lay on the ground row upon row, sometimes stacked two and three corpses high. There were grotesquely deformed testicles between legs, bloated bellies, rotting faces. It was a nightmare vision.

I confess that I could not keep my eyes on the screen. I had to look down at my feet to fight the nausea that was rising in me. After many tortured minutes, my colleague nudged me. He was Jewish. "Let's get out of here," he said, and I was relieved to follow him out of the theater. We rode back to the house in his jeep, silent and looking straight ahead. We went to our separate rooms without speaking of what we had witnessed. Once alone in my room, I could not remember ever having looked at a German while the film was running.

I went alone the second night and stayed to the very end, long enough to see what followed on the scenes of death: there were American officers, faces distorted with anger, looking back over their shoulders, horrified. Then there were German civilians, brought in buses from the nearby town, rows of them being made to walk through the camp. They were ushered by grim-faced MPs in white helmets, carbines across their chests. The contrast between the nearly naked prisoners and the well-dressed burghers intensified the horror. The camera searched the visitors' faces. Some few seemed indignant that they had been brought to the place, one man clearly crying out in angry protest. But most were clearly shocked to the depths of their beings. Men and women alike put handkerchiefs to their noses, while some women wept, shoulders heaving.

As the film ended, I moved into the lobby and stood where I could observe faces as the audience left the theater. It was like seeing the last scene of the film again: there were those who, hard of face, looked resentful. Some women were sobbing uncontrollably. Many women leaned against their male companions, seeking support and comfort. Handkerchiefs were pressed to faces. Not one returned my gaze.

On my third and last visit, two evenings later, I watched only the audience. Their reactions came early: sobbing, moans, choked monosyllables, a loud *"Mein Gott,"* a woman half rising from her seat.

Many must have heard from friends and relatives what they should expect, but the shock wave that swept through the theater that night was as powerful as it had been on the other evenings.

At the end, I again took a place in the lobby, this time standing close to an exit so that I could hear anything that might be said before people could catch sight of me. But there was no talk; they were silent, stunned. All, that is, except a group of uniformed German sailors, members of the mine-sweeping units, who suddenly appeared at the top of the stairs from the balcony. They talked noisily as they descended, causing some in the lobby to look up angrily at them and mutter, as members of a congregation might mutter over somebody violating their sanctuary.

As the sailors reached the bottom of the stairs and turned toward the street exit, one of them gave a loud laugh that rang through the quiet lobby. Thereupon an elderly woman, short and stocky, took off her shoulder the large purse that was hanging by a strap and, swinging it in a large arc, gave the offending sailor a blow on the side of his head so hard that he fell to the ground. Those nearby stopped and clapped their hands, beaming at the woman, then looked threateningly at the sailors, who pulled their comrade to his feet and left the lobby quickly, casting anxious looks over their shoulders at their angry countrymen.

I wish now that I had gone over to shake the woman's hand, but I kept my distance. I was still among the enemy. But as I drove home, I felt for the first time that there was indeed such a thing as a good German.

CHAPTER ELEVEN

A War Criminal

The evil of the Nazi state remains personified for me in the only war criminal I came face to face with. I knew him first as a name on a very short list of those in our territory who were wanted by my government for war crimes. There were three such men, but he was the only one of them thought to be still alive, though missing. A Gestapo member, he was sought by the Royal Air Force for having reportedly murdered many British and Canadian airmen. His name was Werner Zacharias.

I had early established that Zacharias had never applied for a ration card, compelling proof for me that he was not living openly in the area. The German police published daily the name of every newcomer to the community who had registered and been issued a ration card. It was usually a short list, and one we checked routinely. From the police files, however, I had quickly learned that the wanted man's wife was living in Bremerhaven with her parents, and it seemed probable that, if he had survived the war, he would some day come to rejoin her there. Once I had a German car and knew that I wouldn't arouse suspicion, I drove past the house to note its location. I would wait for him to appear, as I felt certain he would.

When a phone call from Hamburg in early 1946 alerted me to the likelihood that Zacharias would be coming home within a few days, I had nearly forgotten about him. The caller identified himself as a sergeant with the RAF commission on war crimes, and he told me that they were particularly eager to catch Zacharias. They knew him from captured Gestapo files as the man responsible for the deaths of thirty-eight airmen. Now the RAF had been tipped that he had been released from a POW camp in Denmark and was likely heading home. I was to let the sergeant know the moment I had Zacharias under arrest. My caller warned me sternly not to let him get away. "This one is a real bastard," he said.

For the next few days I studied the police lists with particular interest and then, one day close to noon, his name was there.

Immediately after lunch, I asked three of the CIC agents to join me, informing them in solemn words what kind of "bastard" we were going to arrest. They were duly impressed and put on their pistols, as I had already done. We went in two jeeps, and then followed the familiar drill: two of my colleagues went to the rear of the house, while the third joined me at the front door.

A startled young woman opened the door to us and acknowledged that she was Frau Zacharias. She led us along a corridor to the rear of the house, where we found her husband in the kitchen, seated comfortably by the tiled stove, wearing civilian clothes and slippers. He was reading the local newspaper, the *Weser Kurier.* He readily admitted his identity, standing up as he did so.

Zacharias was a giant of a man, several inches taller than my six feet two, and broad of shoulder. He would have been a tough man to stop, if he had decided to make a run for it. He said he was surprised to see "both a German-speaking Englander and an Ami" in his home, but he seemed altogether cooperative. He was curious to know why we had come to call; his papers were "in order"; he had been "properly released to come home." What could we want with him?

He was as arrogant in his manner and speech as he was compliant in obeying my direction that he get himself ready to go, and then climb into one of the jeeps. He looked my two colleagues up and down as they came from behind the house, and I'm certain he knew we would shoot him if he were to try to bolt.

When we pulled up before the police building, he said, "So, you are a kind of police." He looked with interest at the "CIC Region IX. Sub-region Bremerhaven" on the pair of glass doors at the top of the stairs and then said, "I used to work on this floor. You are keeping it nice and clean."

My Jewish colleague and I led him to my office, where he again insisted that we had no reason to bring him in; his discharge papers were all in order and he had come home as he had been directed to do. What could we want with him? I told him that he would be taken to Hamburg to be interviewed by officers of the Royal Air Force, but he remained puzzled. "What can the British air force want with me?" he grumbled.

When I told him that he would be charged with the deaths of thirty-eight airmen, he exploded. "No!" he shouted. "That is not correct!" Then, still indignant, he added, "It was thirty-six. I kept an accurate record."

I was astonished at this ready admission. I looked at my colleague, who was clearly as taken aback as I was.

"You are admitting you killed thirty-six airmen?" I asked him.

"Killed? I executed them. They were criminals. I did my duty."

I told him to tell us exactly what had happened.

He explained that, in the last year of the war, he had been assigned go out with a driver to pick up captured airmen. The coast north of Bremerhaven was a fly-over area for the bombers that passed over nightly on their way to Hamburg, Hannover, and Berlin. The attacks on major German cities had been stepped up significantly toward the end of the war, and the Germans had responded by massing anti-aircraft batteries between Bremerhaven and Cuxhaven. Planes were regularly shot down, their crews usually killed in the crash. But occasionally an airman survived, only to be captured quickly by the local police or by angry citizens, who were under orders to turn captives over to the Gestapo. Zacharias picked them up.

Coolly, he told us that, on the trip back to Bremerhaven, he would have the driver stop at a remote spot. Then he would tell the airman to get out to smoke a cigarette. He shot his victim in the back of the head and rolled the body into a ditch. He always made the same report to his indifferent superiors: the prisoner had been shot while trying to escape.

My colleague, flushed of face, said in measured German, "You have admitted that you are guilty of war crimes."

"No, no," Zacharias insisted, "*They* were the criminals. They were destroying our cities. They had killed thousands of women and children. Just look what they did to Bremerhaven. Schools and hospitals . . . . " He spoke angrily as he went on, "If I had brought them to the city, they would have been put on trial and convicted. They would have been hanged. I executed them formally. There was no point in having them tried."

"You have said that you killed thirty-six men, but the records of your office show thirty-eight. Isn't that correct?" I asked after pulling my thoughts together.

"No way," he replied. "Two died of wounds before I could get them into the car."

I completed the arrest report and phoned for two policemen to escort him to the jail. While we waited for their arrival, I phoned the RAF sergeant. He was jubilant. He said it would be too late in the day for them to reach Bremerhaven before dark; they would come by noon the next day. We should hold Zacharias over night, preferably alone in a cell.

The two middle-aged policemen who came for Zacharias looked dubiously at him when they entered my office and received their instructions. Each had a rifle slung on his shoulder, each wore the uniform that always seemed to me to have come from some comic opera.

George, our German investigator, was sitting on the bench in the hall as I led our little procession to the glass doors. With the prisoner safely in the hands of the police, I was on my way to get an arrest report typed up.

George gave me a quizzical look as we reached him. I indicated that he should come into the main office with me, as the policemen took Zacharias down the stairs. He had offered no protest from the moment I told him that he would be held overnight and turned over to the RAF on the morrow.

I quickly told George about the Gestapo man, unable to hide my glee that we had caught him. He raised his eyebrows and whistled. There were two other agents in the office, and I led them, George, and the secretary to a window where we would be able to watch Zacharias being marched off to jail. He was by far the biggest fish we had caught, and I wanted an appreciative audience.

We watched as the trio crossed the intersection, Zacharias towering over the policemen as he walked in step between them and as they moved up onto the Geeste bridge. Then we gave a collective gasp of dismay as Zacharias dropped a half step behind the unsuspecting policemen, grabbed their collars and bashed their heads together. As they fell to the ground he dashed across the bridge and turned right at full speed into the ruined area on the other side. Scores of bewildered civilians turned to look after him, as some went to the assistance of the prostrate policemen.

"Impossible to catch him," George said, but my colleagues were out of the door and running down the stairs in a trice.

George was right. We drove through the bombed area, finding no trace of him in the sea of rubble. We returned to the main office, where others of my colleagues were gathered, discussing what had happened. They turned anxious faces toward me. I was, of course, near panic. I had visions of facing a court-martial for dereliction of duty. I ought to have had the man handcuffed, at least. Better, I should have taken him to the jail in my car, with a colleague pointing a weapon at his back. I couldn't think what to do. My knees were weak.

George roused me, suggesting that we go to Zacharias's home to see whether we could find any clue as to where he might head. I got two of my colleagues to go with us.

It was George who found a letter in a desk drawer, sent to Zacharias's wife a few days before from Bederkesa, a town on the eastern edge of the county. It was from his sister, who asked for news of him. George thought it likely that Zacharias would head there, for he would have to find some friendly soul to hide and feed him. But it was already growing dark, so we resolved to drive to Bederkesa early the next morning. We confiscated the letter and gave Zacharias's wife and her terrified parents emphatic instructions that they were to communicate with nobody. We had not told them of his escape and left them in the dark about the reason for our search of their property.

I decided not to inform the RAF of my blunder. I would pray that I would never have to tell them.

But I found it hard to sleep that Friday night. I was up early the next morning.

George rode to Bederkesa with me, and two agents followed in a jeep. We quickly found the sister's house, and she readily told us that her brother had gone with her husband to watch a soccer game. We spotted him immediately, of course, and, when I tapped him on the back, he turned and smiled amiably. We had no further trouble with him. I said a silent prayer of thanks.

The RAF sergeant and an officer arrived in a Mercedes sedan close to noon that happy day. They were very pleased to be invited to an American lunch at the CIC house, where not a word was said about Zacharias. Then my Jewish colleague joined me in leading them to the jail and getting Zacharias into the back seat of their car, after the sergeant had handcuffed him. He, wise man, told Zacharias forthrightly in fluent German that he would be shot if he tried to escape. The last I saw of him, Zacharias was gazing straight ahead, his face expressionless.

I confessed to my colleague that I was more than relieved to have been able to turn over Zacharias to the RAF men, and that I hoped fervently that they would get him to Hamburg without any trouble.

"Perhaps," he said grimly, "they'll stop and have him get out for a cigarette."

It was several months later that I got a letter from my mother with a newspaper clipping and her explanatory "I'm sending you this because it says the man was arrested in Bremerhaven. I think he's the one you told us about." The clipping reported that Zacharias, a convicted war criminal arrested in Bremerhaven, had escaped from prison in England. But he was spotted by a golf pro who was out practicing on the course early in the morning. When he saw a large man in prison garb running across a green, the pro hid behind a tree and, as Zacharias ran past, felled him by a blow on the head with a club.

Then it was several years before I heard of Zacharias again. By then, in 1952, I was a graduate student at Harvard, where I was working for a Ph.D. in German literature and thought. I found one of my fellows in the staff room one day reading a book on German war crimes, and I asked him whether I might look for mention of Zacharias. I quickly found the entry. The British had put Zacharias on trial, found him guilty, and hanged him. It seemed a fitting end.

I never had any trouble understanding men like Zacharias. The uniform he wore had given him the authority to be a thug with impunity. He was not a stupid man; indeed, he was intelligent and verbally skilled. The Nazis had converted his patriotism into fanaticism and had given him a framework of belief in which he could find justification for shooting unarmed, sometimes wounded, prisoners of war. There were many in Germany like him, alas.

CHAPTER TWELVE

Informants

Americans have learned painfully in Iraq that an intelligence operation that does not have reliable native informants on the ground will be dangerously faulty. At worst it will be useless. Equally, an intelligence organization that does not have people who know the language and culture of the target country will be unable to furnish the intelligence its government and armed forces need. We recognize now how handicapped we have been by lacking people on the ground in Iraq and home-grown experts on Islam and Arabia in sufficient numbers. It is the price paid by a people who have thought of other countries mostly as nice places to visit.

When I joined the CIC unit in Bremerhaven, I had had enough experience with the German language to allow me to do my job without ever having to use an interpreter, but I would have been a much better agent if I had had then the knowledge of German culture and history that I acquired later through my studies. As it was, at first, I blundered every day. How much less effective, obviously, were those of my colleagues who knew not a word of

German! For them it must have been like a tone-deaf person trying to appreciate music.

Intelligence school had taught me that a prime task before me was recruiting *reliable* informants. It was what my effectiveness would ultimately depend on. Reliability was crucial, our instructors had stressed again and again. When we sent in reports that included information from an informant, we were required to rate the reliability of the informant before we assessed the value of the information. That may seem an obvious thing to do, but it is sometimes a lesson painfully learned.

I began to build an informant network, as I had begun other tasks, with information on scraps of paper and names scribbled in notes left behind by the British intelligence team that was briefly in Bremerhaven in the chaotic days at the war's end. Those were in a folder, along with other papers, that Dan Canfield handed over on my second day in Bremerhaven. Then there were the names in Gestapo files of Germans whom the Nazis had suspected of being less than true supporters of the *Führer*, often identifying, as did the notes left by my countrymen, former functionaries of the political parties that, once competitors of the Nazi Party, had been banned altogether in the Hitler years. And I was soon to come to know the names of some who had been victims of Nazi persecution, men who had been cruelly jailed or, in the worst instances, had spent time in concentration camps.

Such a one was Max, a refugee from East Prussia. He had fled with his wife ahead of the advancing Russians, who, they had reason to fear, would not distinguish between Hitler's supporters and Hitler's victims. They were billeted on a farm, located in the northern sector of my county, belonging to a man who had never been a Nazi sympathizer. He and Max had formed a good relationship, a rather rare phenomenon among the hundreds of refugees and those natives who had been forced to take them in. Max presented himself at my office one day not long after my arrival, sent over by the captain at the British MilGov office, where he had first tried to offer information.

Max was my first informant, and the one who served me longest. A man in his early sixties and retired, he introduced himself as a former lathe operator, an ardent unionist, and a minor office-holder in the party called the Social Democrats. He had continued, in his phrase, "to open his mouth" after the Nazis took power, and, following an initial interrogation by the Gestapo and an ignored warning, he spent two years in a camp. (Today people commonly think of the concentration camps as prisons exclusively for Jews. but in some camps Jews were housed with murderers, rapists, political prisoners, and sexual deviants. I came to know others who, like Max, had served limited terms.) We had not conversed more than a minute or two before Max stood up, rolled up his sleeve. and showed me the disfigured arm that was his daily reminder of the torture to which he had been subjected. Max wanted revenge, and he was eager to sniff out Nazis and see them arrested. He offered me his services.

Max was valuable to me in my early months, but he eventually became a liability. He was a simple man, too passionate to be a wholly reliable informant, but he had time to hang about the shops and taverns, initiating or joining conversations, and learning what was on people's minds. He was just as willing to ride his bike over to neighboring communities and plug into the refugee populations there. By doing so, he put me on the track of some Nazi officials who had blended into the local populations but were known to some of the refugees. That he had only a very brief local history, like all the refugees, was of course one of his weaknesses. In time, as the Social Democrats reorganized and became a functioning political party, Max joined and kept me informed about their activities, too. He was a born tattler.

But eventually Max became a problem for me. After a year or so, he identified with me so strongly that he began to attend town council meetings and to claim that he was speaking for the British military. That, of course, was without my authority, and, for some time, without my knowledge. I had a very painful few minutes with a visitor to my office, a banker and town council member, who complained in measured sentences about Max's behavior at their open meetings, his attempts to bully councilors. and his demand that he be recognized as my spokesman. The banker went on to say that we could not hope to nourish a respect for the Occupation and for democratic government, if Max were allowed to continue. I have never forgotten his final words: "I am sorry that you think you must rely on such people in your work."

I called Max in and dressed him down -- that's how good my German had become -- telling him that he must subdue his passion, if he wished to continue to be helpful to me. Max was crushed. I was castrating him. After that, he came less often, but he behaved himself.

The banker was right, of course. It *was* a sorry thing that we had to rely on people like Max, as we did very often. But intelligence work is not a lovely activity. It is a form of police work, and sometimes policemen must turn to criminals for their information. People do not look fondly on tale tellers or rumor mongers; they do not admire snooping and prying; they don't like people who keep track of other people's doings. In intelligence school, I had often found the lectures on informants distasteful, and I had not imagined that I could ever feel comfortable with a person who came to me to denounce a neighbor. But in practice I was comfortable with most of my informants, and I came to think of a few of them as close friends. I never succeeded in my first ambition -- having an informant in every significant town and village -- but in time I was comfortable with the number I had and very confident that nothing of importance could happen in my territory without my learning about it.

As I did all my informants, I paid Max. Rather, I rewarded him and them. The CIC made "confidential rations" available to us: cartons of cigarettes, coffee, candy. I was very frugal, sometimes giving an informant only a couple of cigarettes, but more often a pack. A half pound of coffee was a special bonus, while a Hershey bar was a treat to be cherished. It seems almost absurd to think that there was a time when a man would think himself richly rewarded by being given a pack of Camels, but that was the Occupation, a time of distorted values and shattered symbols of worth.

I never gave an informant a whole carton of cigarettes. But my informants, I must emphasize, with one possible exception, did not give me information or spy on people just to obtain cigarettes. They were nearly always men who were genuinely concerned to help us, whether in the beginning to get known Nazis out of circulation or, later, to support a fledgling democracy. But there were a few like Max, motivated principally by a wish to be avenged, and there was one who acted out of a deep sense of guilt. I shall write of him in the next chapter.

I had my disappointments, of course. The first came when I invited in a couple who had been identified by one of my countrymen as prime prospects, doubtless because a Gestapo file identified the man as a lawyer, a sometime newspaper columnist, and an outspoken critic of the government. He and his wife were brought to my office -- a less risky thing for them than my appearing at their door -- by a kindly neighbor who had a car and a modest gas allowance. They had trouble with the stairs and were out of breath when they reached my office, for they were old and frail. I was quick to fetch them coffee and a cookie from Helga.

The "government" the man had been critical of was, in fact, the government before Hitler, that of the Weimar Republic. In letters to the editor, when he and his wife were still living in Hamburg, he had faulted the government for failing to deal with the extremists of the left and right. By the time Hitler came to power, the lawyer was ready to retire, quickly recognizing the drastic changes in his world. Later, he was able to afford to move to the countryside when the bombing began. Now they lived quietly and at peace with their neighbors, "uninvolved." Sad to say, their son and daughter had both fallen under Hitler's spell, and that had led to rifts. They did not know the whereabouts of either child. The couple could offer their prayers for our success, but there was nothing they could do directly to help.

I had several such disappointments. For some Germans, survivors of a time when the Gestapo had spies everywhere and when children were encouraged to inform on their parents, the idea of being an informant was repugnant. I could sometimes see from the expression on their faces that I had fallen in their esteem by suggesting the role to them. Moreover, they were convinced that the sense of defeat among their neighbors was so complete that there would be no thought of resistance to the Occupation. "Impossible," they would say with emphasis. We didn't recognize then that they would be proven right.

My favorite among my informants was handsome, debonair, sophisticated. In spite of that, he was first-rate. Like the old couple, he was a native of Hamburg who had moved out of the city to a former summer home on a lake, although he took up a new profession at the same time. A man in his early forties, he had once been a successful, versatile actor who had played Shakespeare and operettas alike, but his failure to join the Party had cost him roles. So he decided to exploit a talent and a hobby by becoming a dancing master. He taught classes and held dances in Bremerhaven and in several smaller communities in my county. His work brought him into weekly contact with hundreds of people, and he always listened to his dance partners and pupils. He was made to order. A visit from him was invariably a delight, for he relayed the latest rumors and reported exhaustively on the mood of the population, both young and old. I always gave him a cup of coffee or two, for I wanted to keep him talking about his former life, describing what it had been like to live in Hamburg before and after Nazi rule began. He told me the vulgar greeting that Hamburgers used to hail one another, and he helped me understand the local dialect better. (I was fascinated by its similarities to the Yorkshire dialect that was my first language.)

A friendship between Walther and me ripened slowly. We came in time to trust each other completely, and I learned more from him than from any other what it meant to be a non-sympathizer in Nazi Germany, hostile to the government in every particular.

Before very long. he invited me to his home to meet his wife and children, but I declined the invitation. I was concerned always to keep an appropriate distance from my informants, and I drew the line at any sort of social intercourse. But in our office sessions I shared much of myself with Walther, and he was comfortable enough to ask my age. When I told him that I was a few months shy of twenty-one, he wrinkled his nose and said, "You look a good deal older," Then, after a moment, he added, "You have a difficult job for one so young."

That thought was not new to me. There was not a day when I felt wholly adequate to the job, not a day when I thought myself mature enough to make the decisions I was required to make. I saw the wisdom in the former rule that excluded those under twenty-one from the Intelligence Corps.

CHAPTER THIRTEEN.

A Werewolf

O n many a day in those first months Helga would bring to my office letters from my territory that were variously addressed in German to "The British Secret Police," "The English Officer," or "The Security Office for Landkreis Wesermünde." Rarely would one be sent to me by name. They were nearly always denunciations, nearly always anonymous. They identified people who had been prominent Nazis and yet were still at large. Occasionally, though, a letter would be a plea for help in locating a missing family member. Busy as I was in my early days, I set most of the letters aside in a folder, vowing that I would some day deal with them. But I made a point of always reading them first.

One morning I read a particularly passionate denunciation of a young fellow who lived in a village just outside Bremerhaven. The anonymous writer described him as one who had grown up to become an ardent believer in Nazism. He had been an active member of the Hitler Youth and a recruiter for that organization. For years he was known in the village as a vocal believer in the "German Mission."

Finally, and most damningly, the letter went on, his strong convictions had led him to volunteer to serve as a "Werewolf." The writer ended with the demand that the lad be arrested and imprisoned for a long time.

It was the first time I had come upon a denunciation of a former Werewolf, so I was more than usually interested in the letter. I had, of course, heard about the organization the Nazis had created in the last months of the war, an impromptu enlisting of schoolboys, fifteen- and sixteen-year olds, who would attempt desperately to halt the advance of the invaders. A recruit was given a bazooka and one shell -- and christened Werewolf. He was to lie in wait in a ditch, or crouch behind a low wall, and shoot at an enemy tank when it got to within a few feet of him.

The German bazooka, called the *Panzerfaust*, was a formidable weapon at very close range, useless against a tank at greater distance. It could pierce a tank's armor and destroy its interior, but the man firing it knew that he would get but one shot, for the tank would roll over him before he could reload. It took a true believer to volunteer to be a Werewolf then, so I had to believe that the boy might give us trouble. But the time of tanks rolling in was past, and I couldn't take the time just then to interrogate a sixteen-year old schoolboy. I could understand, nonetheless, why the good folk of his village wouldn't want him around.

Some two weeks later, I spotted an envelope in the little pile that Helga brought that day. It caught my attention because it was addressed in the same purple ink that the writer of the Werewolf letter had used. And I remembered the handwriting. I groaned a little as I slit the envelope, irritated at being prodded, made to feel that I was not paying attention. What I read was the same recital of charges, the same passionate denunciation. But this time the letter was written in the first person and signed with the boy's name, as though the Werewolf were himself asking to be arrested and punished. Goodness, I thought, somebody must really have it in for this kid, to go to the extent of forging a confession. Maybe he is a danger to us. I decided to have the village policeman send him in.

The lad who appeared at my office looked anything but a threat. He was nothing like the Werewolf I had imagined. Tall for his age, gangling, a shock of blond hair, ill clothed, he was chiefly remarkable for his terrible case of acne. He blushed when I spoke his name and invited him to sit down. I could feel the tension in his body, and I imagined he was wondering what I knew about him that would have had me summon him to the police building. But he seemed to fear the worst. All in all, he seemed a pitiful specimen.

I began forthrightly, telling him that I had received an anonymous letter from somebody in his village, describing his passionate support of Hitler. He showed no surprise, not even when I went on to tell him that the first letter had been followed by a second, in which the same author had forged his name to a faked "confession." He was quick to respond. "I know," he said. "I wrote them both."

I was astonished. This was something I had never imagined happening. But before I could ask a question, he went on. "I want you to arrest me," he said. "I want to be punished for all I have done and for all I have believed." He had obviously rehearsed his statement, going on quickly to describe how he had been persuaded that the English and the French had sought to destroy Germany with the iniquities of the Treaty of Versailles. He told me how his teachers had convinced him of the truths of Hitler's preaching. He was intrigued by hearing them tell how the revived German nation would champion the traditional European cultural values that were threatened on the one side by Marxism, on the other by the decadence of the West. The Hitler Youth organization had offered him the opportunity to work on behalf of the "German Mission" to resist these threats to Europe and to create a "New Order" of socialist brotherhood and peace. He had been an idealist, as his parents were, and his patriotic conviction had led him to want to fight Germany's enemies. Still only sixteen, he had volunteered to be a Werewolf.

When he paused in his narrative, I asked him whether he had in fact fired on a tank. No, he had not. He and several others had been taken out on a truck and dropped off singly at what were thought to be strategic points, in his case by a bridge over a stream. He had his bazooka and his one shell, together with a small amount of food to see him through the day. But when night came, nobody had come to pick him up, and so he curled up in a ditch and slept till dawn. After a time some German soldiers came walking along the road and told him that the war was over. He threw the bazooka and shell into the stream and walked home.

He wished me to know that he was deeply ashamed of the beliefs he had held. He and the German people generally had been deceived by Hitler, who had even convinced them that the invasion of Poland had been a legitimate response to the abuse of Germans living in Poland, including the rape of German women. Now he knew that it had been a lie. Hitler's insane adventures had ruined Germany and left the people disillusioned and destitute.

But, he went on, the fact that he now knew the truth should not exempt him from sharing the guilt for what had been done in Germany's name. He urged me to see that he was punished. By this time he was close to tears.

I asked him what had happened to bring about his change of heart, to cause him to recognize that he had been deceived.

Without a moment's hesitation, he said, "The film. The film about the Jews in the camp. It was monstrous. And now," he went on, "our newspaper is beginning to report on Nazi atrocities in the occupied territories, and to tell of the arrogance of our former leaders in denying any responsibility for the horrible things that were done. We must all atone for their guilt."

As I sat and listened to the lad, whom I shall call Hecht, I found myself thinking, "There but for the grace of God go I." What he told me about his upbringing, his hard-working parents, his loyalty to his country, his readiness to believe what his teachers told him, his trusting belief in the authorities, all fitted me. I could think, as I have often thought since, that if I had been born German in 1925, I would have walked in his shoes. I felt a strong sympathetic bond with Hecht, finding myself unable to believe that he was telling anything but the truth. I was equally convinced that he represented no threat to the Occupation.

When he emphasized again his wish to atone by spending time behind bars, I suggested to him that he might instead assist me and others in trying to ensure that his people would never again be so deceived. He had told me that the Nazis among his teachers were gone, replaced in some instances by older teachers who had been forced out by the Nazis. He found no reason to think that there were any believers among the new ones.

After some further conversation, I proposed that he come to visit me regularly each Saturday morning, to keep me informed about his classes and about what was going on in his village. He looked a little doubtful, even disappointed that I was not going to arrest him, but he nodded his assent. I kept him a while longer, talking about the Occupation and about the prospects for a democratic Germany. He was bright, serious, concerned. I was confident that he would make a good informant.

He was to play a key role in helping us deal with the nearest thing to an underground movement Bremerhaven would have.

CHAPTER FOURTEEN

Displaced Persons

It took me quite a long time to understand the dimensions of the "DP problem," as we commonly called the difficulty of dealing with the population of displaced persons in our area. "DP" was a catch-all label applied to peoples of different origins and with various hopes for the future. There were, in fact, large numbers of them in *Landkreis Wesermünde*, as there were everywhere in the American and British Zones of Occupation.

On the one hand, there were Germans from Silesia and other eastern provinces, some of whom had been brought to the county as farm laborers in the middle war years. Far more had arrived in the war's last months, having decided not to stay in their homes and endure occupation by the Russians. They knew that they had every reason to expect harsh treatment from the dreaded Russians in repayment for what German armies had inflicted on the Slavic populations in the countries they had invaded. All of these refugees had been billeted with the native populations, with a resultant crowding that was barely endurable for both sides. I knew of some small farms where there were two refugee families imposed on the farm family.

But we had no problems with the displaced Germans, other than their complaining about their reduced circumstances.

Much more of a problem were the former slave laborers, foreign workers conscripted into factory jobs as well as for farm work. The large majority of these were Poles, though there was a sprinkling from France, Belgium, and Holland besides. The immediate wish of the Allies and of many of the DPs was that they be repatriated as quickly as possible. Most of those from Western Europe were very eager to return home, though some few had reasons to stay on, not least to take advantage of job opportunities with the Americans. A few, I was eventually to learn, stayed on for the opportunities afforded by the black market. I remember one amiable rogue who appeared at my office to propose that we employ him. He was a Rumanian who readily acknowledged that he was a trader in cigarettes, coffee, and anything else that had a value in the marketplace. Well dressed and seemingly well fed, he was touring in the largest car that Opel had built before the war. He spoke atrocious German, equally atrocious English, but he had the self-confidence of the successful con man. He was sure he could be helpful to us -- at a price. He was armed with authentic-looking papers issued in the British Zone that enabled him to move about, apparently without difficulty. He claimed to have been very useful to a British intelligence team when the war first ended. I sent him on his way.

I came to know well three DPs who chose to stay and work for the Americans. One was the Hollander I identified earlier, an interpreter and for a few months the office manager for the unit. He always claimed to have been forced into Germany, though I had some suspicion that he had come there voluntarily for work opportunity and to polish his German. He stayed for about six months before returning to Holland, once he was sure the universities were open again and that he could resume his studies.

There was a Belgian woman who worked on the floor above us, an interpreter and secretary with American MilGov. She was a vivacious thirty-some. I never learned anything of her history, though she visited my office frequently on business and liked to converse with me in French. She stayed in her job with the Americans so long that I wondered whether she was afraid to go home, perhaps having been accused of collaborating with the Germans. At that point, women in formerly occupied countries were getting their heads shaved for such offenses.

Then there was Henri, who was Canfield's sole informant, though a most valuable one. He had been an officer in the Belgian army and was forced into

Germany after his country's defeat, eventually being put to work on the Bremerhaven docks. In due course, he had won the love of a German woman who, by the time I knew him, was his common-law wife. He was utterly opposed to being repatriated, wishing to remain in Germany until such time as he could marry the woman legally. He was counting on Canfield to protect him against the people who were trying to send him back to Belgium. His value to us lay in his continuing to work on the docks, where he picked up talk among the union members, many of whom were Communists. (The Communist Party had been quick to reorganize at war's end, and its local leader was a man who had sat out the Hitler years in Moscow. I often encountered him in the hallway when he was on his way to visit my American colleague who worked in political intelligence.) Canfield always assured us in staff meetings that, thanks to "Henry," as he always called him, we would know at once if the Communists tried to close down the port. They never did, but the threat was always there, and people were still talking about it when I left Bremerhaven in September of 1947. By then, Henri and his legal bride had taken up life in Belgium, and we were relying on one of my informants to keep us abreast of what the dock workers were up to.

Such trouble as we had with DPs came from the Slavs. Officially, we were committed to turning over all Slavs in the Enclave to the Russians for repatriation. I recall vividly a conversation at the dinner table a few days after my arrival in Bremerhaven. Canfield had invited the British MilGov captain to join us for dinner, doubtless to help Garrett and me cement relations with him. But the pleasant mood of the occasion was changed when the agent in charge joined us at the table. Arriving late from a visit to headquarters in Frankfurt, he had scarcely begun his dinner when he declared, "Your government and mine, Captain, have entered into a despicable agreement with the Russians. We have agreed to turn over to them every DP of Slavic origin in our Zones. They will all be murdered."

The captain demurred. "Surely they wouldn't want them back just to kill them."

"Oh yes, they would," the American retorted. "The Russians see these people as traitors, willing collaborators with the Germans. They want them back so that they can execute them. They don't want them left in the West to spread stories about what the Russians have done in Poland and the Ukraine."

In fact, many of the Slavs in the Enclave had come to Germany voluntarily. Many of them had hoped for Russia's defeat. Poles and Ukrainians alike considered the Russians tyrants who, over the history of their countries, had crushed and pillaged them time and again. Even among the slave laborers there were many who feared that to be returned to their homes meant certain death at the hands of the Russians. Some of them were eventually able to find sympathizers among the Americans and British, people in influential positions who enabled them to escape being turned over to the Russians. But most were rounded up and sent back.

That there was such a huge population of foreign workers in Germany during the war was the direct consequence of two of Hitler's cherished convictions. One was that "inferior peoples" like the Slavs were fit only to be slaves, to be forced into the service of the *Reich.* The other, which he could not have held onto without the first, was that married women should not work outside the home, even in wartime. Whereas "total war" in England meant that every woman over eighteen was required, like every man, to be engaged in an activity that supported the war effort directly, in Germany a woman was to be a *Hausfrau,,* center of the home, bearer and mother of children. While England's munition factories were kept running by women, Germany's were manned by slave workers.

There was understandable hatred of Germans among the DPs, though some told me of feeling affection toward the farm families they had worked for. Many farmers treated their foreign workers well and kept them decently housed and fed, sometimes at risk to themselves, for the Gestapo did not look kindly upon soft treatment of slave workers. Those

DPs who sought to avenge themselves on their German masters were a small minority in the population, certainly in our territory.

Early in my time in the Enclave, I heard rumors of DPs raiding outlying farms and stealing pigs or chickens. Nobody made much of that. But there came alarming reports of a farmhouse being set ablaze in the middle of the night, the family perishing. As the report became clearer, we understood that the attack had taken place within the Enclave, but not close to us. Then there were similar stories of arson near Bremen, with a lucky identification of the attackers being made just as they chose to set a house on fire. A boy sleeping in the loft of a shed was wakened by a noise made by the attackers, two of whom he identified as Poles who had worked on the farm. Eventually the gang's hideout was located by an alert German policeman, and the raiders were captured by American troops. The agent in charge of the Bremerhaven sub-region was summoned to Bremen to witness their execution by firing squad. I recall clearly the "before and after" photographs he handed around the dinner table: eight men tied to posts, hoods over their heads. We were under martial law. Justice had been done. Those observing the executions were told that the DPs had readily admitted their acts, believing that they had administered justice.

I heard of no local problems of that magnitude with the DP population after this, although my informants told me from time to time of hearing that DPs were heavily involved in the black market. That was of no concern to us until a colleague who had fled Vienna got wind of a gun-running operation that reached into the Enclave from the British Zone. He showed great courage and initiative in going undercover and posing as a Hungarian DP who wanted to buy weapons. He was so convincing in the role that he was eventually taken to Düsseldorf in the British Zone to meet the head man of the operation, a Polish DP who claimed to be able to deliver anything our colleague might wish to purchase, provided he could pay in American scrip. Only when the deal was finalized did the agent contact the local British intelligence team and have the gang rounded up. He got a well-deserved commendation for his work from Frankfurt HQ. I think his operation the best piece of work accomplished by any member of our unit.

None of us had any idea what our colleague was involved in until he calmly and modestly revealed it in a routine staff meeting after his return. Knowing that his very life depended on maintaining absolute security, he had said not a word to anybody, explaining his necessary absence for a few days by telling the agent in charge that he was going to Frankfurt to discuss the possibility of a job with the CIA after his discharge. When we learned what he had accomplished, I felt for the first time that I was actually involved in a true intelligence agency. Most of the time, I had felt that we were spinning wheels.

CHAPTER FIFTEEN

An Old Trick

The file on the man was enigmatic, to say the least. Every week, letters were coming in from one of the larger communities in my territory, denouncing its biggest Nazi, a former *Ortsgruppenleiter*. His Party rank put him on our automatic arrest list. He ought to have been put behind bars weeks ago. The writers of the angry letters demanded to know why he, a leopard that had not changed its spots, was still running around loose. He was variously described as a liar, a swaggering bully, an unreconstructed Nazi who still mouthed the Party line, and a convinced follower of Hitler who had profited from holding his Party position for a dozen years. Many reported that the man had been so dedicated a Nazi that he used to berate people on the street when they failed to give him the "German Greeting" (right arm raised at a forty-five degree angle in salute), or if they did not enthusiastically say *"Heil Hitler"* in response to his greeting. Virtually every letter ended with the demand that the man be arrested and put away. Our credibility was at stake.

Such letters had come in before my arrival in Bremerhaven; there were samples in the file I had inherited from Canfield. Yet in that same file, governing all else, was a statement from one of my fellow countrymen that Wendell (not his real name) had been released from jail by the British because he had been put there by the Gestapo. He had told his liberators that the Gestapo had arrested him because he had defamed Adolf Hitler in the late days of the war.

At first, I shrugged off the many denunciations as the work of people who were not willing to believe in the late conversion of an erstwhile fanatic, perhaps people seeking to be avenged for the insults and abuse they had suffered, and continued to suffer, at the hands of an instinctive bully. Yet it was puzzling. The Gestapo, I was certain, was too busy to have thrown one of the faithful in jail without good cause.

So, as the letters continued to come in, some of them the work of people who had tried to get our attention earlier, I became convinced that there must be something to warrant my taking a look at Wendell. When I had occasion to be close to his community one day, I decided to drop in and see what the local police officer had to say about him. I had had occasion to meet the sergeant there once before, and I remembered him well: a middle-aged, war-time refugee from the east, a wounded veteran of the Russian campaign. He had been both courteous and helpful on that occasion, and I looked forward to speaking with him again.

The sergeant wrinkled his brow when I told him the name of the man in whom I was interested. He answered cautiously, explaining first that the man was one of the biggest landowners in the district, and the owner besides of a flourishing lumber business. People said that Wendell had made a great profit selling lumber for the buildings at the airport at Nordholz. He had a well established reputation for being a hard-nosed businessman as well as a tough customer. He was a widower, looked after by a daughter who had lost her husband on the Russian front, the woman reputedly as committed a Nazi as her father. Wendell was said to be very resentful over having been obliged to take in two German refugee families.

When I pressed the sergeant for his views on the allegations made against Wendell, the sergeant spoke even more slowly. Yes, he shared the writers' opinion that the former Nazi official continued to be a believer; he himself had heard Wendell talking in the tavern in defense of Hitler's war on the Jews. But he hastened to add that he had no first-hand knowledge of what Wendell had been before the war, and he could not imagine any reason the Gestapo could have had to arrest him. He did know that Wendell boasted of having been given a clean bill of health by the British who had released him from jail, something that most people in the town found impossible to believe. One reason he was gossiped about so much was his reputation for having treated brutally the Polish farm workers he had had in large number. Everybody seemed to know about that. The sergeant thought I should certainly wish to question Wendell, and he volunteered to escort me to his farm. He was pleased to have a ride in a car, he said.

Wendell's place was the most prosperous looking farm I had yet seen. Its appearance bore out the claim of his critics that he had profited from his Nazi activities. We were greeted at the front door by a large-armed young woman who looked resentfully at my uniform, doubtless seeing me as one of those responsible for the loss of her husband. But she answered politely when I asked for her father, telling us that at this time of day he would be at his office at the lumber business. We found him there, working at papers on his desk. He looked angry at the sight of us, but he stood up as we entered.

I disliked him immediately. He was a bull of a man, short-necked, large in the shoulders, with bristled hair, the appearance of a man comfortable with violence. I could easily believe that he had flogged his Polish workers.

I had barely introduced myself when Wendell interrupted me, saying emphatically that he would not speak to me in the presence of the sergeant. When I raised my eyebrows at this, he said that the sergeant was the leader of the pack of refugees who had been forced on the community and who constantly made trouble. They were the ones responsible for spreading evil gossip about him, and the sergeant was the worst of the lot. No, he would not cooperate with me in the sergeant's presence. He flushed red with anger.

I persisted, saying that I wished to ask him a few questions about his being arrested by the Gestapo and subsequently set free by the British. But he shook his head, not hearing me. No, this was his office and he would stand on his right to refuse to be questioned, so long as the sergeant remained.

Then I lost my temper. In that case, I said, I will question you without the sergeant -- in my office. I ordered him to the car, asking the sergeant whether he could make his way back to his office on foot. Wendell looked puzzled and muttered under his breath, but he got into the car without ado. I rolled down my window; he had a foul odor.

Once in my office, I sat him down and put routine questions to him at first, eliciting the response that he had indeed been a loyal supporter of Adolf Hitler, enthusiastically so, until the Allies successfully invaded Normandy. Then he had spoken critically of the *Führer*, seeing that Hitler had failed to heed the advice of his generals and had thus lost the war for Germany.

Somebody had overheard him and informed the Gestapo, and that was why he had spent several weeks in jail, until he was released by the English. He had nothing to hide, nothing to be ashamed of. He was an honest man. I would find nothing in his history to say that he was anything but a true German.

Nothing rang true. I recalled all those accusations, those accounts of his devotion to Hitler and his threatening those who didn't seem to him "true" enough. I was certain he was lying, and yet I couldn't think how I might refute his claims. I took him over the ground again, asking when he first came to his new conviction -- he didn't recall just when -- and to whom he made his declaration that Hitler's decisions had cost Germany the war. He couldn't remember that either. How did people react to his criticisms of their leader's decisions? Oh, he said, they were of like mind; everybody thought Germany could have won the war if the right decisions had been made. Then he paused, perhaps thinking he was going too far. He looked resentful. He seemed startled when I asked him about his arrest. "When did that happen?" I asked. He paused and seemed to consider his answer. "It was at night, after dark," he said finally. That didn't surprise me.

"What did they say to you when they arrested you?" Again a long pause, and then: "I had insulted the *Fuehrer* and I would be imprisoned until the war was over."

The man was lying. Everything in me insisted that he was bluffing, that there was some particular reason for the Gestapo having jailed him. I had a sudden thought.

"I have been told that you made a large profit on your sale of lumber for the new airport," I said, looking hard at him. "The Gestapo found out you had falsified your charges. That is why you were arrested."

He erupted. "That is a lie," he shouted. "I am an honest business man. I have always been that. This is one of those rumors the sergeant and his people have spread about me. There is no truth to any of them." He leaned back in the chair and fumed.

This time I believed him. I had grasped at a straw and it had broken in my hand. I spun my thoughts through the letters of denunciation and through the sergeant's observations. There must be something I could get him to talk about and perhaps have him then trip over his own words. I thought of something else.

"You had many Poles in your employ in the war years," I said. His expression changed abruptly, and I knew I had hit a nerve. He leaned forward in his chair, anxious; he was on his guard now. There was something here that he didn't want probed, but I knew there was no reason the Gestapo would have taken him in just for beating up a slave worker or two. I gazed at him, my mind racing. How could I get him talking? Then I thought of a trick we had been taught in intelligence school that could sometimes catch a prisoner off guard.

I picked up a piece of paper on my desk, a report I had received a day or two before from the German police. It was on official note paper. I pretended to peruse it, letting him see the letterhead, and then said slowly, as though I were having trouble reading the German, "In the matter of *Ortsgruppenleiter* Wendell and the Polish . . . . "

He cried out before I could continue. "*Ach,* you have known all along . . . it was harmless . . . I was a healthy man . . . I had my needs . . . the Polish woman had her needs . . . it was nothing of importance." He began to sob. I didn't ask him to continue. I knew now what his crime was.

It was *Rassenschande,* "disgracing the race," a crime the Gestapo would certainly not forgive, a crime so odious in the eyes of the Party's leadership that not even a loyal servant of the Party could get away with it.

I had a German policeman take Wendell off to jail and wrote up the arrest report with an enormous feeling of satisfaction. Under "Recommendations" at the end, I wrote, "Ask him if he remembers the name of the Polish woman."

Only later did it occur to me who must have turned him in. I thought of the stern, heavy-armed daughter: a true Nazi like her father, the sergeant had said. I knew that she would have been sickened by her father's befouling her mother's bed with a woman of an "inferior" race.

CHAPTER SIXTEEN

The Censors

The British entered Germany having had much experience with the censoring of letters. In wartime Britain, everybody knew it was going on. New recruits in primary training were warned that their letters home would be routinely examined by Army censors, and that material might be excised, if transmitting it were thought to be a threat to national security. It was rumored that censors, stern ladies armed with scissors, snipped out offending passages rather than just blacking them out. The story was widely reported of a woman receiving a letter from her soldier son with "Dear Mother" and "Your loving son" separated by a rectangular hole, while at the bottom of the page the censor had written, "Your son is well, but far too communicative." I have sometimes wondered whether that tale was put into circulation in the early war years by a government eager to have its people know that their mail was being examined. It went along with the ubiquitous posters warning the populace that "Loose lips sink ships."

In the years of the Occupation the censors were not at all interested in having the Germans know that letters they received had been examined. Quite the opposite. Censors took care to conceal the fact, steaming open envelopes and handling the contents with rubber gloves. When a letter roused suspicion, it was copied and then sent on, with the copy being forwarded to an appropriate intelligence agency.

Judging from the steady flow of intercepted letters that were sent to me during the early months in Bremerhaven, our censors' suspicions were easily roused. An inquiry about the whereabouts of an SS unit at war's end might seem to the censor evidence of an SS man's wishing to organize old buddies into a resistance movement. A writer's wanting to know about a certain ship coming into port from New York might be a clue to intended sabotage. Somebody writing a long rant about the awful treatment of German POWs in British holding camps might be a man angry enough to try to organize an underground cell. Might a letter that mentioned a Party leader contain a clue as to the hiding place of a wanted war criminal? The censors were an edgy lot, but it was their job to be suspicious, even paranoid, and to alert us to anything that looked remotely like potential trouble.

Intercepts came to me via our Bremen headquarters, and to that office I responded. I never ignored an intercept, though I never found in one a lead to a threat to the Occupation. In fact, I recall only one mail intercept with any clarity, and that is because it turned out to be not at all what the censor or I could have imagined.

It was a simple, handwritten note, just a few lines long. It had been sent from a remote corner of my county, the work of a girl who seemingly wanted to get back in touch with an old girl friend. "Dear Hannelore," she wrote. "Do you think of me? I often think of you. Do you remember the dances and the handsome boys of the SS? We often laughed together. Think fondly of me. Your Maria." The censor had underscored "boys of the SS" on the copy that came to me and had put a large question mark in the margin. In those early months after the war, any mention of the SS made us nervous, even a seemingly innocuous one, and I promptly asked Helga to phone the policeman in that location and have the girl come in. Then I forgot about the letter and went on to more pressing matters.

One of those involved George, our German investigator, who was in my office when Helga knocked on my door to tell me that the young woman had come two hours before her scheduled time. Could I see her? Mildly irritated, I told Helga to send her down to my office and explained to George what it was about, showing him the note on impulse. The girl was at my open door before he had finished reading it, and I invited him to stay. By that time, I had no secrets from George.

She was a pretty young thing, sixteen or seventeen, neatly dressed, a circle of blond hair about her face, and extraordinarily large blue eyes. She looked bewildered at the sight of me. When I asked her to come in and sit down, she hesitated. Still standing at the door, she said, "There must be a mistake. I was told to come to the American police, but you are an English soldier. I think the English are not our friends." But she sat down, looking nervously at George, who had taken a chair in the corner behind her. "Is that one also an Englander?" she asked.

Not responding to her question, I asked her to tell me about her friend Hannelore.

"Oh, do you know her from the dances?" she asked. "Do you still go to the dances?" I didn't need George tapping his finger to his temple to tell me what the girl's mental state was.

I told the girl to remain where she was and opened my door, intending to tell Helga to get the girl to a hospital, but I found a stiffly dressed, middle-aged woman standing in the hall. "Are you perhaps with the girl?" I asked. She explained painfully that she was a worker in the mental hospital at such-and-such a place (I had not known of its existence to that point), and had brought the girl in, following the instruction from the police. She had asked the secretary to have me see the girl early, because they had to take the only train back at the time the girl was scheduled to see me. She went on quickly to say that she and her superior had been quite unable to understand what I could possibly want with this girl, who had lost her mind after being raped by a gang of SS trainees a year ago. "She has been in that state ever since."

I took the woman into my office, apologizing for an obvious and unhappy mistake on somebody's part. Not knowing how else to make amends, I pressed two Hershey bars on the woman and asked George to drive them to the railroad station in my car. As he took the keys from my hand, he muttered, "The handsome boys of the SS!", snorting his contempt.

CHAPTER SEVENTEEN

The Black Market

Every Friday evening, a pleasant, middle-aged German was present for a couple of hours in the bathroom on the first floor of the CIC house. He was there to cut the hair of any agent who wished to be served. The barber spoke next to no English, so I was often called on to explain to him how a newcomer to the unit wanted his hair styled. Once told, he needed no reminders. The charge for a haircut was a few German marks and two cigarettes. For that, I got the best bargain in haircuts I have ever had. If the barber was engagingly gossipy when he cut my hair, I tipped him a third Lucky Strike. He had a silver cigarette case into which he put his precious take. He had, of course, given up smoking.

That's the way it was with every transaction between Americans and Germans, Germans and Germans. While the essentially worthless German marks gave the transaction legal status, the real payment for service or for something purchased was in American cigarettes. The economy of the Enclave was a cigarette economy; the only vital market was black.

There were, of course, efforts made and measures taken to control activity in the black market, far more vigorously in the American Zone than in the British. The outlawing of real dollars and the use of scrip exerted some control; a GI could not send home in a money order an amount greater than his pay in the period since his last transmission. There was a limit of two cartons of cigarettes per week that could be purchased at the PX. It was a crime for a German to possess scrip, improper for a GI to have German marks. Open trading of cigarettes could lead to arrest and punishment, for Germans and Americans alike.

But there were enormous pressures on both sides to engage in trade. Sometimes it seemed as though all of Germany were for sale, and every American a buyer. GIs coveted Luger pistols as souvenirs, and Germans always had them to sell. Leika cameras, gold watches, jewelry, porcelain, silverware, crystal, china, books, art works, German shepherd pups, everything could be had for a price -- above all, women. The price would be quoted in cigarettes: by the carton, by the pack, by the single cigarette.

One could not live in the Enclave without being drawn into the trading. I paid in Camels and Lucky Strikes for the German suit and shirt I had made. I fed the market indirectly with the cigarettes I provided my informants. And, worse, I sold cigarettes for both German marks and scrip, with our houseman Adolf as my agent.

I had begun fairly innocently. A heavy smoker in our unit asked me to sell him a carton he knew I would not smoke. Following my practice in selling Scotch, I charged him twice the price in scrip that I had paid at the PX. He was delighted, since he knew what that carton could have fetched, had I given it to Adolf to sell. Before long it was the Hollander, the Belgian woman, and Canfield's informant Henri, smokers all and without access to the PX; they begged me to sell to them. That wasn't really *black* market trading, but it wasn't really honest either. Then, perhaps inevitably, I wondered whether those who bought from me were subsequently selling in the market for prices far higher than mine, profiting in a way at my expense. I decided to have Adolf get me the scrip for one carton each week. I knew that would allow me to live very comfortably, even while I had the British Army paymaster sending all of my modest pay to my mother. She banked it for me and I felt virtuous that I was saving. But I was officially a crook.

I have salved my conscience somewhat by being able to say that I did not buy on the black market. No cameras, no Lugers, no art works, no women. I had no part in the looting of Germany that went on. Well, that is not quite true, I now recall. One day my mother, who had repeatedly urged me not to be tempted to buy things on the black market, wrote to ask me to find a pair of German razors -- "slashers," she called them, to identify the instruments she meant. She wanted them for a brother-in-law who had a notoriously heavy beard that couldn't be controlled by the miserable razor blades available in England. He had assured my mother that the German products were peerless. I never told her that the boxed pair I carried home with me on my next leave had been paid for with American cigarettes.

And then there was my complicity in a clearly illegal transaction. At the request of one of the later agents and after his departure, I shipped to the States a set of sterling silver cutlery he had bought in the black market. He didn't have room for it at the last minute when he packed for home. Some customs officer in New York must have decided it was loot, for the agent never received his purchase. We had heard that things were being confiscated when it was obvious that they were black- market purchases. Meanwhile British troops were being shown on newsreels happily pushing down gangplanks baby carriages filled with loot, as they disembarked for a leave in England. Or, again, they were shown exposing an arm that displayed two dozen watches or more. Perhaps the British, after years of austerity, thought that they were more deserving of reparations than the Americans.

It had all seemed fairly harmless so long as there was a sense of tit for tat and wasn't plain looting, with everybody getting something out of it. But then, one day in 1946, it suddenly turned very serious. The new agent in charge asked me to have a private chat with him in his office; it was a matter, he said, of some delicacy.

He explained that he would like me to take on the investigation of an unidentified American soldier, whom the German criminal police suspected of being a kingpin in the black market. The agent in charge thought that my being British would let me be a thoroughly detached investigator, and that my doing the job, rather than an American, would help persuade the German police that the charge was being taken altogether seriously. I agreed to do it, though made slightly uncomfortable by the passing thought that the German police might think their man was one of my CIC colleagues.

I began by listening to what the head of the German detective unit had to say on the matter. It wasn't much, other than that one of their informants had repeatedly told them that an American with some access to port installations was bringing in large quantities of cigarettes and was using his gains to buy real estate in Bremerhaven. I decided to get George to work on their suspicions.

Using his contacts in city hall, George soon learned that the mayor of the city had recently performed a marriage ceremony between a German woman and a man who, though he spoke Austrian German, was thought to be an American masquerading in civilian clothing. (At the time Americans, military or civilians, were forbidden to marry Germans.) George was even shown a copy of the license, which identified a bridegroom with a name that could be German or American. No good evidence there. The man's declared address was that of the bride; his occupation, clerk.

From another source George learned of a major real estate transaction, the recent sale of two apartment houses to a woman whose name was the same as that on the marriage license. The sellers were identified as two German physicians, partners in general practice. We decided we should pay them a visit to see what we could learn about the purchaser's identity.

George knew the two doctors by reputation, for, though not themselves prominent Nazis, they had rubbed shoulders with the Nazi elite in Bremerhaven. He had not known that they owned apartment buildings, though he could imagine that they might have made profitable deals buying real estate hastily sold off in 1936 by fleeing Jews. He was very eager to have at them.

Their circumstances now much reduced, the physicians shared offices, even as they shared a dwelling. Their bank accounts had been blocked because of their history as Party supporters, and, George proposed, they could have consequently been eager to get their hands on some money and have been ready to sell property, particularly if some American scrip were involved. I had George make an appointment for us to visit them after their office hours.

It didn't take us long to get them talking, and they readily acknowledged that they had been present when the ownership of their apartment buildings was transferred to a woman of the city. I asked whether the woman's husband was at the transaction, and they acknowledged his presence, one of them noting that the man had remained silent throughout the occasion. He had merely nodded his head when they were introduced by their attorney. "Could he have been an American?" I asked. They looked at each other and shrugged noncommitally. George pulled out a piece of paper on which he had noted the price paid for the properties, and asked the doctors what they had received in payment. They looked very uncomfortable at this, but quoted the figure George had, to which he said, "Correct," letting them know how well informed he was. Then, ingenuously, he asked, "And what in scrip beyond that?" Both flushed at the question, knowing they were on thin ice. To admit that there was American money involved could convict them, but they couldn't risk a denial, since they didn't know what else was on George's piece of paper. They quoted a figure that was 20% of the official sales price. It was a figure equal to many, many cartons of cigarettes

We decided to visit the woman's apartment that very evening and hope to find the soldier there. We did. He was helping to put her two children to bed. He was in uniform, wearing the insignia of his unit and corporal's stripes. He was very, very surprised to see us. His "wife" had lost her husband in the war, "fallen in Russia," but now she thought herself legally married again and the joint owner of a considerable property.

It was the CID's business now. My task was done. The next morning, I made my report to the agent in charge, and then to the German police. The corporal's name and the information we had gleaned about him were given promptly to the CID, for the German police had no authority to arrest an American.

Things moved swiftly. The agent in charge got word from his counterpart at the CID that the corporal, a native German speaker and a refugee from Austria, had imagined that he could take up residence in Germany after his honorable discharge. Then he would be able to live a very comfortable life with his wife and children on income from his properties, for the apartment buildings were not his first purchase. He had planned to hide his purchases and bring no suspicion on himself by putting all the property in the woman's name. He thought he would be excused for a marriage that would be only temporarily illegal in American eyes and was already legal in Germany. I never knew or was able to guess whether he had first fallen in love with the German woman and only later thought of real estate deals that would allow him to live well in Germany with her and her children, or whether he had first thought of becoming a German property owner and then found a woman whom he could use as a vehicle for his scheme.

The CID head had added that the corporal would certainly face a court-martial back in the States -- he had been quickly put aboard a troop ship -- and would likely serve a considerable prison term. But I never heard another word about the case, and I made no attempt to check on the woman's fate.

I did make sure that George transmitted all we had learned about the corporal's activities to his German contacts. We were never able to discover how he acquired the cigarettes necessary to his operations. Talk of an American heavily involved in the black market soon evaporated.

CHAPTER EIGHTEEN

Operation Nursery

T he largest and most sweeping operation I was ever involved with had its origins in the British Zone. There an informant had turned over to an intelligence agent the extensive files of an organization that had been brought into being in the final days of the war by henchmen of Heinrich Himmler, the head of the SS, a close colleague of Hitler, and the most feared man in Germany, whose instructions were to be obeyed, no matter how extravagant they might seem. Himmler, having recognized that Germany was suffering overwhelming defeat, had evidently called on his underlings to create the cadre for an insurgent group that would wear down the Allies, causing them to tire of the Occupation and to leave Germany. Then, he evidently imagined, the seeds of a restored Nazi state would sprout.

Himmler did not live to help revive Nazism. Like Adolf Hitler and Josef Goebbels, he committed suicide in the final days of the war, while their colleague Hermann Goering took his own life only after he had played games with the prosecutors and judges at the Nuremberg War Crimes Trials.

Himmler had been caught at war's end on the German side of the Danish border, trying to reach an escape route that would have eventually landed him in Argentina, where other Nazi bigwigs did in fact find refuge. But Himmler's attempted escape was foiled when an alert British sentry spotted a quartet of suspicious-looking men sitting at the curb in the sort of car the Nazi leadership favored for parades. As the minutes ticked by and the car remained where it was, the sentry guessed that the men were waiting for the final rush at the last second before the border closed, when screening might be superficial. He called them to his sergeant's attention, and that good soldier promptly arrested them and turned them over to a British intelligence team.

Knowing that the jig was up, Himmler was at once cooperative with his captors and talked freely with the officer who questioned him about his identity. But that officer, once he learned what a prize catch he had, followed orders and summoned an Army doctor to examine the prisoner. The doctor, told who the prisoner was, immediately began to abuse Himmler verbally, promising him swift and drastic punishment. At that, Himmler bit down on a poison capsule he had concealed in his mouth, and was dead in seconds. (I had the story directly from a sergeant on the intelligence team.) Needless to say, Himmler would have been a goldmine of information about the Nazi years.

So used had we become to the compliant ways of the civilian population in the several months since the war's end that we were utterly astonished to be told of a planned insurgency. We got the news at a special staff meeting to which both my boss, now promoted to captain, and the new agent in charge of Region IX came from Bremen. I joined my American colleagues of the sub-region in the office of the agent in charge, also a newcomer, to await the visitors.

That office, large and luxurious, had reminders of its former Gestapo occupants. There was a foot of insulating space between pairs of windows, and double doors with heavy padding on their facing panels. It was a soundproof room, appropriately so given the top secret information we were about to be given. There was plenty of space for all of us to sit comfortably -- and expectantly. We had had time to speculate endlessly about what this special meeting was to be about since having been told of it a couple of days earlier. Most speculation had centered on the CIC being converted to a civilian organization. We had all guessed wrong.

The Region's head man began with a warning that not a word of what we were about to hear could leave the room; it was top, top secret. Then he introduced my boss, who had visited the sub-region only once before, in our first days in the Enclave, so he was an unknown quantity to nearly everybody in the room. But he quickly held everyone's attention with his solemn delivery. What he briefed us on was the evident setting up of an underground organization of members of the Hitler Youth and its companion girl's organization, the *Bund deutscher Mädel*, whose members were chosen for their utter commitment to Nazi ideology. They were people who might have been instructed to lie low until the call came for them to organize resistance cells, or perhaps they had previously been trained in sabotage to be directed against certain critical installations (we all thought immediately of the port of Bremerhaven). Information was sketchy, the captain continued, since the informant had produced not much more than lists of names and addresses of people in every sizable community in Germany.

"Operation Nursery," as the plan to destroy Himmler's scheme was called, would cover only the American and British Zones, for both the Russian and French intelligence communities were not considered secure.

On a certain night two weeks hence, between midnight and five in the morning, every person named in the lists would be arrested. We were to take in those in our territory and deliver them promptly to Bremen for interrogation. We were not to question them. It was crucial that not one of them have warning of what was to happen, so only one person of those present at our meeting would be entrusted with the names of the suspects in our territory. Because the operation had begun with the British, the captain went on, it had been decided that the operation in the Enclave would be under his overall direction, while in the sub-region it would be in the hands of Warrant Officer Haywood. (I, too, had risen in the world.)

I was stunned; my stomach shrank; I am certain I must have blushed deep red. My colleagues shot looks at me, some of them sympathetic.

My boss went on, "I am turning over to Mr. Haywood a sheet of paper with six names and addresses on it. Between now and the time for the arrests he will have to ascertain whether the people are in fact at those addresses. He will not reveal those names to anybody else." At the meeting's close he handed me a sealed envelope and, smiling, said, "Don't let this out of your sight."

I didn't need any further warning to tell me that this was serious stuff, and that any misstep could ruin the entire operation. I was terribly, terribly anxious. As we adjourned, a couple of my colleagues commiserated and offered their help, but they knew that the buck stopped with me.

From the moment the captain had mentioned the Hitler Youth, I had feared that Hecht's name would be on the list, and I was utterly relieved to find that it wasn't. I guessed that he had been thought too young for a leadership role. The three men on the list and two of the women were in the city; the third woman was in an outlying community. She might be a problem. It would be easy enough to check on the presence of those within Bremerhaven, for the German police had accurate, up-to-date housing lists. But I wouldn't dare to consult those in the file room with Germans about. Playing safe, I had the police deliver to my office the files for all the streets in the town, not just the five streets where my targets were thought to be. I gave no explanation for why I wanted the files, promising only to return them quickly. Two burly policemen, tunics off, brought up box after box, and I was pleased to see that every box had the initial letters of the streets in the box marked in large red letters. From there on it was easy. Three of the targets lived in apartment buildings, the others in houses; all lived with their parents. The curfew would ensure that all of them were at home and in bed during the wee hours. But I worried. I needed somebody to share my worry.

I enlisted the help of the agent who had rediscovered his German while working at my elbow. From the beginning I had imagined his leading one of the two teams we should have to have, if we were to get the arresting done within the hours scheduled, particularly with the girl out of town to be reckoned with. So, without revealing any names to him, I had him join me in checking out the places where the targets lived. Like me, he had acquired German clothes, and we used my car to give us further cover. We drove slowly down the streets, checking numbers, looking at entrances and exits. By the time we were done, I could feel confident that the operation in Bremerhaven would go forward without a hitch.

I had to think very carefully about the country girl. I couldn't possibly go to the policeman in her community and ask him to tell me where she lived. Nor could I ask to see files at the mayor's office, lest somebody gossip about my interest. It was a top, top secret business and I couldn't take the slightest risk. I wouldn't even risk driving out there in my car, in case somebody were to remember having seen it before and talk in the tavern about me.

Fortunately my colleague had acquired a grey Wanderer that he had never taken out of the city. So one afternoon he drove us out in the car, and we toured several streets in the town, noting the house we wanted to spot. Given that the Bremerhaven housing lists had confirmed the addresses I had been given, I could reasonably hope that I would find the girl at the address I had for her. And that she would be home in bed.

At the staff meeting before the critical date, I explained my plan to the group. We would have two teams of four men, each team to use two jeeps. Another agent would stay by the phone, just in case a call from Bremen came in. We would begin immediately after midnight, with my team taking the two who lived in suburban houses, the other the three apartment dwellers near the city center. Arrestees would be handcuffed to jeeps; they would not be permitted to speak to other arrestees. All were to be delivered promptly to the German jail, where I would arrange for them to be placed in solitary confinement until we could transport them to Bremen.

With the arrests in the city completed, we would return to the house, and I would then take my team out into the country.

My two arrests went off smoothly, although we had to endure protesting fathers and bawling mothers. The male looked bewildered, still half asleep, anything but the tough guy I had thought we might find. The young woman, who insisted on having time to put on make-up. was the hard case I thought she would be. She was scarcely in the jeep when she demanded a cigarette. One of my colleagues whispered that she must certainly be a GI's girl friend.

Waiting back at the house, I was a little worried that the other team seemed to be taking a long time. My mind sifted possibilities. But eventually we heard noise at the front door, and they were jovial as they saw us sitting in the living room drinking cups of coffee. I looked inquiringly at their leader, the last to enter. "How did it go?" I asked, though I hardly needed to put the question. He laughed at once, his companions smiling.

"The first two were a piece of cake," he said, "but then we got to this apartment, where the woman told us that her daughter wasn't home. I told Joe to check the bedroom, but the mother was telling the truth. The father yelled at him. I asked the mother where the daughter was, and she said she was with her boyfriend. When I told her to give me the address, she got all coy. So I told her I would take her in, if she didn't come up with the address."

The other agents of his team were grinning broadly by now. He continued, "So we get to this address on *Hafenstrasse*, and it's the bachelor officers' quarters." He paused for maximum effect before telling me that the American who opened the door to their loud knock was the occupant of an office on the floor above us in the police building. Loud laughter all around mixed with anxious feelings on my part as I waited for the outcome.

The officer had refused at first to believe that the CIC could be serious in wanting to arrest his girlfriend. "She's a good kid," he repeated over and over. "I've known her for months." But he got nothing out of my colleagues as to why she was being taken in. The scene had ended with the girl weeping profusely and the officer choking on his anger and frustration.

With that behind me, I took off for the country with my group. A very young girl answered my knock and my *"Aufmachen, bitte. Polizei."* She was startled to see that we were not the German policemen she had expected to see. Our uniforms must have alarmed her, for she set up a wail. I could see that she had risen from a sofa that was her bed, but, just as she was acknowledging her name, a woman, evidently her mother, pushed her aside to confront me. She was outraged and demanded to know what we could possibly want at her door. She was not easily calmed, insisting that her daughter, still a schoolgirl, could not possibly be of interest to the occupying powers. To her protests against our presence she joined her anger at having two refugees billeted on her, a pair of elderly brothers who had come down the stairs and were standing uncertainly in the little hall at the foot of the stairs. My colleague shooed them back upstairs. The girl followed my instructions and dressed quickly. Her mother followed us to the jeeps and continued her harangue as we drove off with her sobbing daughter.

I arrived early at my office the next morning, after a very short night, and was barely finished with my telephone call to Bremen to report our success, when there was a knock on my door, and the officer from upstairs entered. He was already flushed with anger, having drawn a blank with the agent in charge, who had referred him to me. I had a very difficult time with him, the more so when I let slip that his girlfriend was not the only one to have been arrested in the middle of the night. A mistake on my part.

Several weeks passed before I heard from my boss that the prisoners were all being released. Not only those from the Enclave, but everywhere in the two Zones. Interrogation had produced nothing. Not one of the arrestees had had a clue about an underground organization, a conspiracy, a list of potential colleagues, or anything else. The "organization" was a figment of Himmler's underlings, a throwing together of names culled from Hitler Youth and BDM membership lists with no obvious basis for the selections. They had to have something to show their dreaded boss. It was a paper insurgency, the only one we ever had.

But I learned lessons from it. The country town where the schoolgirl lived was also home to one of my best informants. He told me shortly after her arrest that the whole community was up in arms about it. He had not seen such anger over any issue since the war ended. People were saying that the English and Americans were no better than the Nazis, hauling people off in the middle of the night. The girl's mother, a Party member of long standing and a notorious loudmouth whose late husband had been in the SS, was known for her Nazi convictions, but the girl was an innocent, a church-goer, a top pupil. His own daughter was the girl's friend, and he knew her well. He couldn't think there could be any reason for my interest in her. At that point, of course, I couldn't tell him a thing, and so I said only that the reason would come to light eventually. As he went on talking about the community's reactions, he referred to the girl's mother by her first name. It was the same as the daughter's.

Then I knew I had arrested the wrong Inge. It was the mother I should have taken in. I couldn't bring myself to acknowledge my mistake to my boss, and I hoped fervently that my suspicions would turn out be correct, namely that none of the persons we had arrested was a conspirator. My boss's report on the release of all the arrestees and their ignorance of any plot took a huge weight off my shoulders.

CHAPTER NINETEEN

Denazification

I have known people to snicker at mention of the word "denazification," apparently thinking that it was used in 1946 to mean something like "detoxification," a treatment of an individual's addiction to Nazi belief. But in fact the denazification program, to use the full term, was our effort to cleanse the German state of Nazism, to rid western Germany of all traces of Hitler's *Reich.* Its obvious manifestations included the outlawing of the swastika and other Nazi symbols.

For the Bremerhaven intelligence unit, denazification translated particularly into our being required to screen all the white-collar people who had been allowed to continue in their positions after the war, as well as those who were applying for reinstatement after their Party membership had caused them to be dismissed from their jobs. It was a task we turned to only after we had pretty well cleaned up the automatic arrests and could think that the most immediately dangerous Germans had been taken out of circulation. Only then did I find myself interviewing doctors, lawyers, pastors, teachers, municipal employees -- all those people who had been obliged in 1936 to join the Party in order to practice their profession -- if, that is, they had not previously joined out of conviction.

It was only then, in 1946 and 1947, that I found myself facing what I will simply call "the educated Nazi." Werner Zacharias and his fellow thugs in uniform were uneducated and unsophisticated men. Whatever influence they might have had on the lives of post-war Germans was quickly dissipated, as more and more people came to understand the brutality of the Nazi regime. What remained was the risk that the educated among the Nazi believers could continue to shape Germany's life and keep Nazi ideology alive. In the long run, it was more important that we remove such persons from positions of authority and influence than that we catch former concentration camp guards.

My interrogation of these professional men and women always began with the questionnaire they had completed and submitted before their appearance at my office. (Everybody, Germans and Americans alike, called it by its official name, the *Fragebogen*, the German word for questionnaire.) Its many questions elicited information about the respondent's person and professional activity, but they particularly sought out the facts of the person's relationship with the Nazi state. My first interest was to see whether answers I got in the interview conflicted with those written responses, a clue to me that the person had something to hide. It was rare that I found any disagreement. I always had the upper hand in such an interview, for the person on the other side of the desk never knew what information I had that wasn't in the *Fragebogen.*

Many, indeed most, of those interviews were pleasant, for the majority of the people I saw had either been neutral toward Hitler (truly apolitical), or had lived quietly and secretly in opposition. They saw their Party membership as a "union card" and no more. I emphasize again that Nazism never had the hold on north Germany that it had on the southern part of the country.

But there were true believers among them, of course. I began to think that I could spot them the moment they began to talk, for theirs was a choice of vocabulary, an edgy awareness in their way of responding, a style of over-answering the simplest of questions, that pointed to my having reason to suspect them. Such men and women I encouraged to talk more freely by misleading them as to my own sympathies. For example, when they justified their support of Hitler's invasion of the Soviet Union, I might agree that that had been initially a good thing, given the threat of Communism to the civilized world. They would be seduced into revealing more than they had intended about their belief in the "German Mission" or their anti-Jewish sentiments. One lawyer began by telling me how pleased he was to find me in British uniform; he had feared he would be questioned by an American. "The Amis," he said scornfully, "have no culture." He went on to speak of the need for a "resurrected" Germany to join with Britain to resist the "democratic" influences the Americans were seeking to spread in Europe. Perhaps made a little dizzy by the Lucky Strike I pressed him to smoke, he went on to give me a lecture on how misguided the British had been not to have sought a peace with Hitler after their defeat at Dunkirk; that would have freed the German general staff from worries about a second front when they were developing their plan for the defeat of the Russians. How much better things would have turned out, he concluded exuberantly, if the German invasion of Russia had succeeded!

It was out of such encounters that I first began to shape a question that was to occupy me for many a year: what explained the fact that millions of people, very well educated by my standards of the time, had embraced Hitler's immoral preachments, supporting the measures against the Jews, believing the Aryan myth and the idea of a German master race? What impressed me time and again, as I listened to the German intellectuals I interviewed, was the absence in their statements of any mention of right and wrong, of good and evil. Their judgment as to the morality of a matter seemed to rest solely on its fitting the assumptions of Nazi ideology. The end always justified the means. There was no such thing as a standard against which Nazi conduct had to be measured.

My study of German literature and thought has persuaded me that Nazi ideology was nurtured by the amoral tone of German intellectual life in the nineteen-twenties and -thirties, and that Germany's intellectuals, above all its professoriate, prepared the ground in which Hitler's ideas flourished. For the Nazi intellectuals I interviewed had studied in Germany's celebrated universities and had there acquired their practice of divorcing questions from a moral context.

The German universities won their reputation in and after the great age of revolution that saw far-reaching political change in North America and France, the beginnings of the industrial revolution in Britain, and in Germany an intellectual revolution to match the Renaissance. Germans have often been credited with accomplishing the intellectual and artistic breakthroughs that have defined the modern age. The ferment that brought forth so much of modern science, modern philosophy, and the Romantic movement in the arts emerged in what had been regarded as the most backward place in Europe. "Germany" then meant scores of kingdoms, principalities, and dukedoms where some dialect of German was spoken and the German of Martin Luther read. More of a common denominator was a medieval social system with brutal political repression. It was dangerous to speak or write of liberty.

It could be dangerous in the universities, too, where new ideas were pushing aside traditional notions and where inherited practices were being challenged. To protect themselves against the clerical and secular authorities who would have condemned them, university faculties declared themselves to be apart from their society. They let the walls of their studies and laboratories surround them (an idea mocked by Goethe in the opening monologue of his *Faust*), and insisted that their pursuits had no extramural implications. They were engaged in the pursuit of knowledge for its own sake, in value-free inquiry. They focused their energies on limited topics of inquiry, seeking "the truth within the discipline." Thus secured and thus focused, German scholars made remarkable breakthroughs in virtually every sphere of intellectual activity; there is scarcely a modern discipline that does not honor a German as its high priest.

It seems not to have been apparent to those in Europe and America who spoke admiringly of German achievements that German intellectual life in the nineteenth century and afterward was marked by its separation from the social and political. Neither do they seem to have been aware of dangerous undercurrents in German thought, particularly in the philosophy of Friedrich Nietzsche, whose voice by the end of the century was the most powerful in the German academic community.

Nietzsche had enormous influence on generations of those who passed through the universities, and it is not difficult to find parallels between Nietzsche's preachings on morality and Hitler's theories of master and slave peoples. In his famous essay "Beyond Good and Evil" Nietzsche argues that "good" and "evil" are necessary concepts for the mass of humanity who are incapable of independent thought. A society will need such concepts to preserve order and civility; the common people can be taught them in their schools and churches. But the independent thinker will wish to be free of such limiting notions. He will advance "beyond" them and create his own notions of what is permitted him and what is not. In a sometimes vulgarized and popularized form, Nietzsche's ideas swept the universities, where "good" and "evil" had already been set beyond the walls. How seductive it was for young men to think themselves the masters, how easy to be contemptuous of the ignorant masses who had to be led by the nose.

I have long since rejected the oft-asserted argument that Hitler corrupted the universities and forced himself upon their faculties. Those faculties proved, in the main, eager to expel their Jewish colleagues and to support Hitler in every way they could. And not just the scientists, architects, and physicians, whose work for the Third Reich has come under scrutiny. Their colleagues in the humanities had created acceptance of amorality in intellectual life; it was but a step to denying a moral dimension to political and social questions. The universities and Germany's intellectuals had prepared the ground for the seeds Hitler would sow across Germany. They formed the vanguard for the idea of a German "mission."

The most important and most challenging aspect of the denazification program was to restore morality to German public life. The program did not wholly succeed, though Germany today, I would certainly argue, is as moral a country as any other in the west.

CHAPTER TWENTY

My Americans

My two years in Germany were the foundation of all my future life. Not only because my experience there led me to seek a career in German studies, but because Bremerhaven proved to be the gateway to my becoming an American citizen. As I think back on those two years, I can see that I spent nearly as much time learning about Americans as I did about Germans. Even as I was becoming fluent in the German language, I was embracing American English and American ways.

I had thought that I knew a lot about Americans before we went to the Enclave, partly because I had been an enthusiastic boyhood reader of Mark Twain and James Fenimore Cooper, even more because of the extensive reading I had done as a teenager on jazz and its origins. Not to mention, of course. those many, many movies I had seen that I naively took to be mirrors of life in the States. I quickly found that those early impressions were nearly all based on false assumptions, the most misleading being the one held by the majority of English people at the time, namely that the United

States is essentially "England at a faster tempo." Another assumption I had embraced -- and had somewhat painfully to release -- was that Americans universally admired the English and had wished to come to Britain's rescue after Dunkirk.

I had two great surprises in my early days that powerfully shaped the new sense of Americans I acquired in Bremerhaven. The first was learning that all Americans spoke the same language and were always able to understand one another. To somebody coming from a land where dialect differences were so great as to make oral communication difficult between people from counties a mere hundred miles apart, that was truly astonishing. To be sure, I recognized that there were regional accents; I quickly heard the differences between Canfield's Kansas speech and the New York-ese of the agent in charge. Later, I would have colleagues from Georgia, Wisconsin, California, Texas, Michigan, New Jersey, Alabama, each with a distinctive intonation, but always at once understandable. I was slow to comprehend that the differences in the linguistic shapes of British and American English speak to fundamental societal differences. England is sometimes strangled by its history; this country never seems to be. Here, mobility has always been prized; in England, rootedness has more often been celebrated.

My second discovery was American generosity, something I encountered at every turn. I think of "Can I help you?" as the characteristic American question. No memory of my time in Bremerhaven is more strongly etched on my memory than the sight of GIs coming out of the PX and dispensing candy and gum to waiting German children -- the children of yesterday's enemy. Like so many pigeons gathered about somebody with bread crumbs to scatter, the children would swarm around the Americans as the soldiers and sailors came out with their purchases. (Two MPs standing guard at the entry insured that there would not be a similar swarm of black marketeers offering to buy cigarettes.)

The children, some of them toddlers accompanied by older siblings, had a litany that they chanted in a chorus of high-pitched voices: "Give candy, Joe . . . Give chocolate, Joe . . . Cigarette for Papa, please . . . ."

Prepared for this, the Americans always had Hershey bars, Baby Ruths, Oh Henrys, and Chiclets at the ready. I never saw a GI push a child aside, never saw one angered by the pestering. And pestered they were. The children had learned to stuff their pockets and save treats till later, even as they had learned to move quickly from a soldier who had exhausted his handouts to one just emerging from the PX. Hungry pigeons have no loyalty.

I must here comment on my own visits to the PX, for once again a deeply etched memory emerges as I recall the first time I entered the Aladdin's cave that was the PX. To understand fully what my astonishment was then, you would have had to live through the nearly six years of Britain's war-time rationing. Those years had made me accustomed to austerity with a capital "A", to living with the barest of necessities and altogether without luxuries. Everything, it seems to me now, was rationed in those dark days. And then suddenly the bright lights and opulence of the PX! It was a while before I learned that the initials stood for "Post Exchange," the place where money (scrip) could be exchanged for all kinds of goodies. In addition to the stacks of cigarette cartons (two per person per week), boxes of cigars, soft drinks, candy (one could buy *boxes* of Hershey bars and the like), there were desirable items from Switzerland: watches of course, cuckoo clocks in an amazing variety, music boxes, jewelry (a sign urged guys to buy something for "the girl back home"), and much else. The Swiss were enjoying the spoils of neutrality. There were nice little American radios; I bought an Emerson on my first visit, as well as a step-down transformer that allowed me to play it on the higher German voltage.

Eagerly waiting upon all who came to buy were German girls who had at least a smattering of English. (They were usually startled when I spoke to them in German, and they viewed my British uniform with suspicion.) Uniformly they were young, over-rouged, over-lipsticked, over-mascara-ed. The young CIC agent who introduced me to the PX was convinced that every one of them had a GI lover who provided the make-up. I never knew whether their extravagant appearance was management policy or whether the girls thought they were emulating American fashions.

I visited the PX at least once a week and never ceased to wonder at its offerings. The day would come when the first products of the restored English automobile industry would be offered for purchase through the PX, and, some months later, there were some of the first Volkswagens to come off the rebuilt assembly line in Wolfsburg. For me, entering the PX every week was like Dorothy in "The Wizard of Oz" moving from black-and-white Kansas into multicolored Oz.

It was when I was coming out of the PX one day that I saw a GI drunk on the street in mid-morning. It was the only time I ever saw an American drunk in public. Worse, this man was also disorderly. He was swearing at Germans who passed him as he staggered along, and then he began to berate an elderly man who had momentarily barred his weaving path. As the German sought to pull away, the GI swung a fist at him, striking him on the shoulder. But in that very moment, as though summoned by the dismay of those of us who were watching the unhappy scene, a jeep roared up to the curb and two MPs leapt out, grabbed the GI, and hustled him into the jeep, roaring off again to the applause of the Germans. I have remembered the scene with clarity because such behavior was so atypical.

From the very first I got along well with my American colleagues and, indeed, with all the Americans I encountered in those two years. In fact, I became so much a part of the unit that, when my boss proposed to move me down to Bremen and replace me with another Brit, the agent in charge made a formal protest, and the captain yielded. Then there came a day when I decided to stay with the Americans rather than accept a promotion to lieutenant that would have meant my being assigned to some place outside the Enclave. That wasn't just a decision to stay with the wonderful food and the riches of the PX; it was my recognizing the extent to which I had become alienated from my native land and had embraced those American ideals that made me wish to become a citizen of the republic.

Most of my American colleagues were interested to learn from me what life in Britain had been like during the war. A few Americans I met had known firsthand, having been stationed in England before D-Day; they were duly sympathetic. Interestingly, they would tell me, after they got to know me well enough to be comfortable saying it, that they felt more at home in Germany than they had ever been in England, notwithstanding (or perhaps because of) the fact that they could usually understand the natives in England. At first I put that down to the fact that Americans and Germans drive on the same side of the road, use knives and forks in much the same way, drink the same kind of beer, prefer coffee to tea, and the like. I didn't know then that the largest ethnic group in the United States is German, or that German immigrants shaped day-to-day living in America far more than the English did. Indeed, the German influence has been so pervasive that one observer has described America as a German country where English is the official language.

My American colleagues were uniformly perplexed that the English had kicked Winston Churchill out of office in the first election immediately after the war. They didn't understand the British parliamentary system, which had required Churchill to resign when his party was defeated in the general election. The English were bitter about the Conservative Party's failure to respond to Hitler's behaviors -- ironically enough, ignoring Churchill's repeated warnings -- and about Britain's having been utterly unprepared to fight a war. It was a failure the electorate would not forgive. But Churchill, who had always enjoyed a better press in America than in England (where he had been labeled a warmonger), was an icon to the Americans I knew, a symbol of gallant resistance and the will to win. Even after my explanation, they shook their heads in disbelief.

My colleagues were united too in their joy that the atomic bomb had ended the war in the Pacific. Those who knew about the scope and cost in blood of the D-Day invasion could say with utter confidence that an invasion of Japan would have been far more costly in lives, Japanese as well as American, than the bombings of Hiroshima and Nagasaki had been. But Japan seemed a very long way distant, as did the Pacific theater of war, and that part of World War II was rarely a topic for table talk. We were focused upon Germany and our role there, though with the passing of the months there was ever greater conviction that there would be trouble with the Soviet Union. It was common gossip even then that the Russians had snatched some of Germany's leading physicists, particularly rocket scientists, even as everybody knew of the remarkable weapons the Germans had unleashed in the final weeks of the war: the jet fighter, the V1 and V2 rockets. So there was often solemn talk after dinner about the threat Russia would pose. I was sufficiently convinced that Russia was going to be the prime target of British and American intelligence that, thinking of a possible career in that field, I resolved to teach myself Russian. That I thought I could do, after having had formal instruction in three foreign languages. I asked my mother to send me a copy of *Teach Yourself Russian*, and I worked at the first few chapters assiduously for a while. But I recognized I was not going to make progress unless I devoted far more time to the study than I had available, and so I abandoned the effort.

My first close American friend was an agent fifteen years my senior. Ed Vande Castle, always called Van, hailed from Green Bay, Wisconsin, where he had worked as an insurance investigator. He knew no German, but his experience made him a very successful CIC agent, and he was soon entrusted with ticklish cases involving members of American units. His tour of duty roughly coincided with the year 1946, a time when I, well settled in with the Americans, displayed an insatiable curiosity about America that Van did his best to satisfy. We were both compulsive letter writers, I to my parents and school friends, he to a new wife and his virtually orphaned children. Of an evening, our letters done, we spent hours together having a quiet beer and talking. Van personified all that I have come to think of as the essential American virtues, and no man has ever been a better friend to me.

In a way, he was the antecedent of Sergeant Gretchen Shelley, whose linguistic skills led to her being assigned to our unit. She was not our first WAC. Helga had been replaced, when anxieties grew about German citizens working in sensitive American offices, by a highly competent typist who knew not a word of German. Our new sergeant's first words upon meeting me, when she was but a couple of days off the boat, were, "Kind of weird here, don't you think?" By mid-1946, I had ceased to see Germany through the eyes of a critical visitor, and I remember feeling a little hurt by her remark. Sergeant Shelley was in no way repelled; Germany was for her a chosen object of study.

Two and one-half years older than I, Gretchen seemed to me far more mature and sophisticated in her thinking than I was. I was intimidated by her at first, recognizing that her language skills, including her knowledge of English grammar, surpassed mine. She had grown up half-English, half-Dutch, in a Michigan community where every friend she had was the child of first-generation immigrants who continued to speak their first language at home. Gretchen had an uncanny ability to absorb a new language just by being around those who spoke it, and over the years she had picked up a conversational ability in French, Polish, Croatian, Dutch, Swedish, and, most remarkably, Finnish. But no German. She was eager to learn German, and had volunteered to serve in Germany so as to have a first-hand opportunity. But she had enlisted primarily because she was so very much a patriot. She wanted to be in on the war, and she had chafed at the rule that kept women out of the service until they were twenty-one. The moment she set foot in Bremerhaven, she set to learning German, and by the time she left a year later she was having easy conversations with the German maids at the hotel where the WACs lived.

Soon after Gretchen joined the unit, the agent in charge found himself facing a demand that he produce a weekly report on the sub-region that would be sent first to Bremen and then to headquarters in Frankfurt. He proposed to Gretchen and me that we produce that weekly report, and so we began a perhaps peculiar courtship, spending every Friday evening together in my office. There we sifted through the reports the agents had turned in, reviewed her notes on the weekly staff meeting, and incorporated whatever I had gleaned from my informants. Love has blossomed under stranger circumstances, I'm sure.

Gretchen took Van's place as my chief source of knowledge of things American, while I was able to tell her a lot about Britain and Europe she hadn't known. It was a bonus that she looked like the young Ingrid Bergman. Eventually, in June of 1947, we obtained our army's permission to marry, and a few weeks later we both enrolled at the University of Leeds in Yorkshire. Gretchen could have been happy living in England, with the access to Europe's languages that would afford her, but I could not settle back into English life. I had served at the King's pleasure for four years, but now I was done with him. I was through being a subject. I wanted to be a citizen.

CHAPTER TWENTY-ONE

Edelweiß Piraten

Those who know Rodgers' and Hammerstein's "The Sound of Music" are happily familiar with the word *Edelweiß,* the name of a little white Alpine flower that serves as the title of one of the best known songs in the production. Indeed, it is so familiar that the former song leader at my Rotary Club often introduced it as a "German folk song."

For me, the word has a less happy connotation, for it was adopted by a "pirate" group that planned to kill my CIC colleagues and me. To paraphrase Dr. Samuel Johnson, there is nothing that will concentrate the mind more than knowing that you are on somebody's hit list.

We first heard of the *Edelweiß Piraten* in late 1946, when Canfield reported at a weekly staff meeting that his Belgian informant, Henri, had told him of hearing a group of young men in a tavern singing Nazi songs. Nobody thought much of that; sticks and stones might break our bones, but singing songs couldn't hurt us. And we had no idea then that they were an organized group with a menacing name. However, the agent in charge suggested that

Canfield have Henri and his wife visit the tavern regularly to see what he might be able to overhear, without it becoming obvious that he was observing them.

A month or so passed without much being added to Henri's first report, other than that there seemed to be a group of about twenty regulars, seventeen and eighteen year-olds perhaps, with a middle-aged man usually in attendance at their weekly gatherings, presumably some sort of mentor. That there was such an adult presence made the group's meetings the more suspicious, but we still continued to watch and wait. At least, Henri watched, while we waited.

Then one of my colleagues, whose office had a window on the street side of the police building, noticed that young men seemed to be taking turns standing on the opposite corner and observing the comings and goings at our front door. They made no effort to conceal themselves, simply standing for a half hour or so, sometimes being relieved by another young fellow, sometimes not. Eventually, he established that their schedule was on Tuesday and Thursday afternoons, and he estimated they were spending three hours watching on those afternoons. They did not gaze intently. They looked about, walked a few steps away, came back, not remaining more than a minute or so in their look-out position. However, it was clear that they were engaged in routine surveillance of those who used the building. It could be us.

Hearing this, the agent in charge said, "These could be the same punks who are singing Nazi songs in the tavern." That thought had crossed my mind, too. Then he said what I'm sure most of us were thinking, "We need to find out more about those guys." And after a pause, "Anybody know how we could infiltrate that group? Anybody know a kid of that age?" He looked around the room, but nobody spoke or raised a hand.

After a moment of quick thought, I said, "I can talk to one of my informants who might be willing to try it."

To that point, I had told none of my colleagues, not even Van, about Hecht. Protecting informants' identities was a routine matter, but, more to the point, I had formed a true friendship with Hecht. I had grown fond of him through our chats at regular meetings, more and more seeing my alter ego in him. I didn't reveal his name now, saying only that he was a former Werewolf who might have contacts in the group. I told them of his eagerness to help us; that might translate into willingness to take on the role of infiltrator. But, emphasizing that I couldn't promise anything, I said straightforwardly that I would have to make sure he understood the risk he would be taking if he were to try to win the group's acceptance. There were looks of expectation and some relief on my colleagues' faces.

When Hecht came to my office on the following Saturday morning, I chatted with him for a time before I broached the subject of the pro-Nazi gang. He listened with growing attention as I talked of their continuing scrutiny of people entering and leaving our building, and, when I paused, he said quietly, "I could try to get to know who they are." That is what I had hoped: that he would volunteer without my having to suggest he attempt to infiltrate. I spoke carefully about the risk he would be taking. If they were the fanatics they might seem to be, I said, they would not shrink from murdering anybody who betrayed them. He nodded his head thoughtfully, his face altogether serious. He had once been a fanatic among fanatics; he knew the kind of people they might be. "I know how they talk," he said. "I used to talk that way. It will be easy for me to convince them."

It was the last time Hecht would come to my office or see me in uniform for a long time. It was obviously dangerous, if the watchers were in fact members of a pro-Nazi gang, for him to be seen coming into our building. We couldn't risk one of them spotting him by chance. So we arranged a location where I could pick him up and then drive out to a place where we could talk unobserved. That became our pattern for so long as I was seeing him.

We agreed on a strategy. Hecht would visit the tavern on the evening the gang regularly attended and would sit at a table close to the entry, where he would be spotted by anybody coming in. But he would not face the door, lest it seem as though he were waiting for somebody. If a fellow Werewolf spotted him, he would surely stop to greet Hecht and, perhaps, invite him to come and have a beer with the group. Above all, Hecht should not seek to rush anything. He would learn what he could by listening and without asking any questions.

It worked just as I had hoped it would. Hecht had not been at the tavern very long before he felt a tap on his shoulder and heard his name called. It was a lad who had undergone the brief training with Hecht before the war ended. It couldn't have been a happier coincidence for us.

His friend urged him to go to the rear of the tavern, where others soon joined them. There were no more Werewolves among them, but all of them welcomed him enthusiastically, once he was introduced as a former Hitler Youth leader and Werewolf. His credentials couldn't have been better. And of course he knew and at once used the Nazi idiom that the group still employed. It wasn't long before they let him know that they planned sabotage against the Amis and that they would soon have weapons. They believed that others would soon emulate them and that the Americans would be driven out of Germany.

I had urged Hecht not to be tempted to ask for any information and to find an excuse to leave early, once they were comfortable enough with him to invite him to join them again. He must not seem to be seeking to find out about the members and their intentions. But sitting with the group over a glass of beer, Hecht quickly learned that they called themselves the *Edelweiß Piraten* and wore a little metal *Edelweiß* on the reverse of their coat lapel. The *Edelweiß* has a history in Germany and Austria as an emblem of resistance groups -- something their leader would presumably have known. The man was not there that first evening, and there was no mention of him.

Hearing Hecht's report the next day, I was immensely relieved that everything had gone as we had hoped, and that we had evidently accomplished an infiltration. Hecht readily convinced me that we had to take the *Piraten* seriously. They were angry, frustrated, and still convinced believers. If they did succeed in getting their hands on weapons, they could be very dangerous, indeed.

The following week the leader appeared about half an hour after the group had assembled. Hecht knew him at once. He was a former teacher at the *Gymnasium* Hecht had attended, one of the convinced Nazis who had been removed from his position. Once others had vouched for Hecht, the teacher accepted him into the group formally and promised him that he would have a part to play in the coming defeat of the Occupation. He made no mention of weapons, nor of any specific targets for sabotage. The talk that evening was mostly about German girls selling their bodies to the hated Amis, and about the various problems the gang members were having in coping with their circumstances. There was no mention of their watching the police building.

Hecht got into my car the following week with the look of one who had something special to tell. Indeed he had. On the previous evening one of his comrades had triumphantly produced a piece of paper on which he had written my name and the names of my American colleagues. He had entered the police building at a quarter to eight one morning, telling the policeman on duty at the entrance that he had been ordered to report to the American secret police. The policeman told him to go up to the second floor, where the lad simply walked the corridor and wrote down the names he read on the doors. The excited talk that followed on this bravado report made it obvious that the gang members were, in fact, those who had been watching our comings and goings. Then the leader intoned solemnly that these secret police must be the first targets for assassination, once they had their weapons, and that observation should continue so that they could be sure of their identification of us. They already referred to me as "the Englander."

My report on this at Monday's staff meeting caused more than a stir. There were those who favored an immediate raid on the tavern by the MPs and the arrest of every member of the gang. But the agent in charge argued successfully that we should wait to see what Hecht could learn about the weapons cache the leader had spoken of. I said that Hecht seemed to have no anxieties about his meetings with the group, and that I thought we could be confident he would let me know immediately, if there were any reason for a quick action against the gang.

A couple of weeks passed with nothing new from Hecht, but then he reported that the teacher had revealed that there was a hoard of weapons in an outbuilding on his father's farm, which was now being operated by his younger brother. He was having difficulty trying to manage the move of the weapons from the farm into the city, where he had found a secure hiding place for them. There was no vehicle at the farm that could be used for the task. But he hoped soon to find a trustworthy trucker who would take on the job. He spoke, exciting his hearers, of ammunition, carbines, pistols, light machine guns, grenades. There was further intense talk at the meeting about the need to make a first assault and the desirability of striking at the CIC, perhaps by burning down the house. (By this time we were all in the one dwelling.) Hecht had not picked up before then on the fact that they had been observing our house, too, presumably hidden in the ruined mansion across the street. One of the gang had rhapsodized about the idea of the gang members circling the house and throwing grenades through the windows to start a blaze and then shooting anybody who tried to escape the building.

But the leader had not told the group the location of the farm.

I reported privately to the agent in charge everything that Hecht had told me and suggested that we bring George in on the case. I thought that, provided the name of the teacher, he could use his contacts to locate the farm, and that this could be a first step to involving the German criminal police in the matter. The agent agreed that I should brief George in his presence.

Within a day, George had located the farm. It was on one of the main roads in the county, and I must have driven past it a score of times without having any reason to give it a second look. From that point forward, the agent in charge took over, arranging for the MPs to raid the farm and for the German police to round up the gang members at the tavern at the same hour. He informed the other agents only after the raid was successfully brought off. I had decided not to go along on the raid. The cache contained all that the teacher had told his pupils, enough ammo and weaponry to start a small war, plus three motorcycle wheels. I have always been puzzled about them.

Canfield had sometimes been ridiculed behind his back for his obsessive belief that there were caches of weapons hidden about the countryside waiting to be used against us by insurgents. Now he felt exonerated. He claimed more credit for Henri in the operation than the Belgian deserved. I continued to keep Hecht's identity a secret.

Like his fellows, Hecht was held in the Bremerhaven jail for several days. Then all were released, for the agent in charge and the criminal police accepted my argument -- properly, Hecht's conclusion -- that the gang would pose no threat without its leader. The teacher was moved to a place in the British Zone where he was tried and jailed for a term. His father and brother, who convincingly pleaded no knowledge of what the locked building on their property had contained, were kept under observation for a time.

The *Edelweiß* affair, in some ways the most engaging case I was involved in, had come to an end. But for Hecht it was a beginning.

Some weeks after the operation, one of my colleagues approached me, asking whether I thought Hecht would be willing to be put on our payroll as an undercover operative. What he had in mind was penetrating the Communist-dominated union at the port. It would be a very dangerous assignment, for, as the agent put it, if they suspected him, they would put a stevedore's hook in his belly and toss him in the Weser. I chilled at that image, but, having had my confidence in Hecht confirmed by his role in the *Edelweiß* affair and knowing his continuing wish to serve us and his country, I said that I would certainly ask him.

Hecht asked for time to think it over, but then decided to take on the assignment. He ceased to be my informant and was successfully run by my colleague and, after that agent left for the States, by another very good agent. I worried about my friend and missed my contacts with him. My colleagues occasionally gave me reassuring news of him, without telling me what he was doing. Whatever it was, he was pleasing them greatly.

Two weeks before I left Bremerhaven, Hecht surprised me by coming to my office on a Saturday morning, as he had been wont to do months before. He brought me a farewell present, having learned from my colleague that I was going to be leaving. It was a small brass anchor mounted on a plastic base. His father had made it for me. After a while we shook hands solemnly and said farewell. He had taken no small risk in coming to see me. I never saw him again. I knew better than to write to him later, for the agent who was his runner when I left told me that he was hoping to infiltrate Hecht into the Communist Party hierarchy. I have kept him fresh in my memory, and I have hoped that he has had a good life. We are in his debt.

CHAPTER TWENTY-TWO

Those Who Came After

The American agents I knew in my first few months in the Enclave were to a man veterans of the war, some having served in North Africa or Italy before moving into Germany. They were older than I, a couple of them by just a year or two, others ten or more years my senior. All had been affected by the war in one way or another. They were serious about their work, understanding what was at stake in Germany, though they were not uniformly successful at what they did. A few carried deep resentment out of their wartime service, usually against the enemy, but sometimes against what they considered gross incompetence on the part of superiors.

Once the war was over, they were eager to return home, and, compared to the British, they were quickly rotated, with nearly all of them gone by late 1946.

Canfield was one of two agents I knew who elected to become members of the new civilian intelligence agency that replaced the wartime OSS. Dan went home on leave and returned after a month as a civilian. He brought with him a brand new

Oldsmobile sedan that held everybody's interest for a time, not least the Germans'. It was one of the first models to come off the revitalized assembly line, a pre-war design, but with a new feature that fascinated all the car buffs in Bremerhaven, including me: an automatic transmission. Canfield was generous in taking groups of four around the town to show off his vehicle's wonders and to let us all experience the remarkable fact that there was no clutch, no gears to shift. Among the beat-up German cars and the tired jeeps, the Oldsmobile was a marvel. Canfield boasted of having connections back in Kansas that had allowed him to get a much coveted new automobile in a car-hungry America.

He had also brought back a new wardrobe, and from that point until his departure for reassignment in Frankfurt, he was resplendent in colorful -- and hopelessly inappropriate -- clothing. He eventually bequeathed Henri, who was still fighting repatriation, to another agent and went his way, to be quickly forgotten. For the unit had a short memory.

As men left and were replaced by newcomers from the States, the character of the sub-region changed. There was far less seriousness to its tone, much more mirth at table, a lot more goofing off. By early 1947, we had more agents by far than we had had a year before -- so many, in fact, that there was doubling up in bedrooms, even on the top floor, where I had had the whole floor to myself for many weeks. My seniority allowed me to remain alone, and I was happy for that.

Those who came later had had no direct experience of the war. They showed no signs of its having affected them, though they had complaints about the minimal rationing that had obtained in the States. For whatever reason, whether younger men just out of college or older married men, they had had deferments, and they came to us knowing that their tour of duty in Germany would last less than a year. For some, it seemed like an extended vacation away from whatever circumstances they had left behind. They arrived eager to learn what was available for their pleasure, be it opportunity to travel about Europe, the black-market price of desirable items, or the availability of women. For the one thing they had certainly heard about in their orientation program was the rush of German women to embrace Americans. And every one of them seemed to have come with a camera and yards of film on which to record the ruined land for the edification of the folks back home. It was my ready impression that they spent more duty time around the city taking pictures than they did in their offices. In part, that was because we now had more agents than we could use, with automatic arresting behind us and virtually no evidence of resistance to the Occupation.

There was one agent, newly wedded, who had evidently brought a list of items his wife wanted him to bring back to her. He was always on the lookout for silverware, jewelry, antique furniture, French perfume, and, above all, china. His pursuit even led him outside the Enclave into the British Zone, following leads some black marketeer or another had given him. His roommate complained frequently about the amount of stuff that was crowding their room, to the point that the agent in charge urged him to be a little more discreet. It didn't seem to slow his pace.

There were those, on the other hand, who sought no contact with Germans or German properties whatsoever, beyond the infrequent encounters their work might entail. Those agents lived within an American "ghetto" that consisted of the house, the office, the officers' club, the PX, the movies, and perhaps, if they were Protestants, the Sunday morning service in the movie theater. (The Catholics, at a time when the mass everywhere was conducted in Latin, went to services in a German church.)

Some in this category seemed to have no idea at all of the circumstances of the Occupation, expecting to live as they had lived at home, protesting when mail was late in delivery, complaining about the poor phone service, annoyed that the electric razor they had brought from home wouldn't work on German current. Least of all did such men understand the still straitened lives that

Germans -- and other Europeans, including my parents -- were living in 1947. I remember one of them, an agent from Alabama, lodging an entry during the complaints-and-suggestions part of our staff meeting. It was a time when there was a dock strike in New York, and shipments to the U.S. forces in Germany had been restricted. "Several times lately," he said, "we've been given just one egg for breakfast. Can somebody set the chef straight? Nobody eats just one egg for breakfast." I had to bite my tongue.

The year 1947 also brought us a supply officer, an entity we had never had before. Suddenly, we were being told that we had to fill out requisition forms for confidential supplies. We could no longer amble down to the main office and pick up cartons of cigarettes, half-pound bags of coffee, or candy for our informants. Did some higher-up perhaps believe we were using them for black-market deals? A little later, we were told that we had to fill out the supply officer's forms reporting how we had used the confidential rations, naming the informants who had been given them. That brought a challenge in staff meeting from one of my colleagues, who spoke advisedly of the need to keep the identities of informants confidential, if not secret. The agent in charge found a compromise in allowing us to use a code name for an informant, but we had to fill out the forms and report precisely the number of cigarettes we had given, to whom, and for what reason.

Bureaucracy was beginning to lay its heavy hand on our freewheeling operation. Who cared about such stuff, I wondered. One encounter I had with the supply officer made me think that it was nobody but the supply officer himself, a lieutenant transferred from a supply unit who had learned such behaviors before coming to us. I asked him one day for a red pencil, only to have him demand to know what I was going to do with it. He gave it to me reluctantly.

This supply officer, an affable man despite his seeming wish never to supply, was the first in our unit to bring his family from the States. By the time his wife and children arrived in 1947, there were many American families in Bremerhaven, some of them occupying quarters in what was known as the "Dependents' Hotel," far more of them in houses and apartments that till then had been occupied by two or three German families. Needless to say, this brought an outcry from the already hard-pressed German civilian population; it was not quieted by their being pointedly reminded that the German army had displaced French civilians in Paris, for example, in order to quarter German families.

The number of new American cars on the streets increased dramatically, as did the demand for German nannies, English-speaking or no. I was much entertained by being in the company of little Americans who, having spent many of their daylight hours with German maids while their mothers were playing tennis, bridge, or what have you, were becoming fluent in a language that was somewhere between American English and German. They seemed to use whatever word they found most pleasing or immediately available to them. I remember hearing, for example, "Look out the Fenster, Papa" and "Want Schockolade, Mommy." "Milk/Milch," "Water/Wasser," "Door/Tür," "open/offen," were easily and understandably interchangeable, and a child might use both in the same sentence. I have often wondered how many of those children remembered any of their German after returning to the States.

As Europe began to move slowly and often painfully into post-war recovery, there were opportunities for Americans, both bachelors and men with families in Germany, to travel and sightsee. It was easy to take an overnight train to Munich and the Bavarian Alps. The much damaged Autobahn stretches were being swiftly repaired, and that allowed officers with American cars to reach Bavaria easily, too. When a stretch of Autobahn to Bremen reopened, Van and I decided to bring up the motorbikes from the basement and take a ride along the road, just to see what a limited-access highway was like. We cruised along, foolishly bare-headed and without gloves or other protection. It wasn't long before we decided to see just how fast those Norton bikes would go, once they were really warmed up. When I got mine just past sixty the bike developed a speed wobble, scaring me and causing me to close the throttle quickly. The bike righted itself, and I turned and drove home at about twenty-five miles per hour. It was the last time I rode a motorcycle.

That outing now seems to me to have been part of a new spirit that was slowly coming over the land, the feeling that the time had come to burst out and ignore restrictions, for new life to emerge from the basements, notwithstanding any risks.

The presence of American families contributed to the sense of a new age beginning -- the New World coming to visit the Old, so to speak. I was pleased to receive invitations to visit my married colleagues in their new homes and to get a glimpse of domestic America. We had two or three childless wives coming to the CIC house for meals on a regular basis, although none was ever housed there. I found them pleasant company and very different in so many ways from English women. Conversations with them across the dinner table contributed to my ever- growing understanding of matters American.

But the sense of change in the air was not always comforting, and I felt a growing unease about what was happening in the unit and in Bremerhaven.

CHAPTER TWENTY-THREE

A New Day

The end to non-fraternization, a rule that was being observed only in the breach by the time it was rescinded, was the mark of a new day in American-German relations. It was followed not long afterward by the lifting of the ban on marriage between GIs and German girls, and that brought new interviewees to our office in droves. There were so many of them, in fact, that the agent in charge asked my assistance in screening them, though they were officially no business of mine. They were would-be brides, anxious to have the knots tied before their fiancés shipped out.

Suddenly, we were swamped with the *Fragebogen* of German women whose GI boyfriends, enlisted men and officers alike, had proposed marriage. The U.S. government, of course, wanted to be sure that no former Nazis were allowed to wed unsuspecting Americans, so CIC was called upon to inquire into the history of the women, most of whom were too young to have had much of a history. But not all were eighteen- and nineteen-year olds. There were women in their twenties and thirties, although I recall none older than that. Some were war widows, eager now to embrace a new life with a former enemy. One or two were divorced. But most had never married. They were a mixed lot, a true sampling of Bremerhaven's womanhood, educated and uneducated, pretty and plain, comfortably off and poor in the extreme, but all alike in wishing to leave Germany as soon as that could be arranged.

Every one of those I questioned was surprised that an "Englander" was doing the screening. They asked me whether there was a particular reason for that, and they often seemed doubtful when I said that there was not. All were terribly apprehensive that some little aspect of their life might prove to be an obstacle to their escaping from Germany. With the image of bustling New York or Golden California before them, and the ruins of their homeland still piled around them, their anxiety was understandable. Almost never did I find anything in the *Fragebogen* they had had to fill out that suggested any political grounds on which to recommend either denial of permission to marry or even caution on the evidence of lingering Nazi sympathies. It was some other officer's job to counsel the would-be husband about the wisdom of marrying a woman from another culture. (It would have been hypocritical for me to have attempted that, since I was by then about to take that very step.)

Taking those women through the hoops of an interrogation was the dullest work I ever did, and it convinced me that I should never become a bureaucrat. But the women caused a lot of talk among my colleagues. Some were plainly offended that Americans were marrying Germans, when the memory of the concentration camps was still fresh. Some were concerned that the women were seeking a comfortable life away from the ruins rather than a loving marriage. The Southerners, and most of the rest for that matter, were appalled that there were German women seeking to marry Black Americans, since we suspected that they would quickly seek a divorce once they got themselves into the States. It was the only time in my two years that I recall after-dinner conversations turning on the day's work.

But all of this was a sign of the change in the mood of the Occupation. Germans were thinking of getting married, not of shooting themselves. There were faint stirrings of a German economic recovery. Gradually at first, things were working more efficiently. One could hope to get a phone call through to Hamburg, say, without it taking the entire evening. There were fewer times when the electricity went off. My informants reported a more optimistic mood in the population. There was talk of the need for a new currency that would surely be forthcoming. People said that they could begin to imagine what life in Germany might be like, once industry really got going again and there was a good harvest. But such talk was always tempered by the fear that the Americans would pull their troops out and leave Germany to be overrun by the Russians. Any gain by the German Communist Party in a local election sent a shudder down German spines.

By early 1947, it was clear that there was no thought of Germany returning to Nazism or, indeed, turning to extremism in any form. The political parties of right and left were moderate and speaking responsibly. There was such a new note in the air, in fact, that I began to think that I might find a career in Germany, whether as a civilian employee of the U.S. Military Government or as a teacher after I had returned from earning a degree in England. I have often had reason to regret, in fact, that I didn't remain in intelligence work for three or four more years.

None of us, when we first saw a Volkswagen Beetle, realized that we were observing what would become the emblem of a remarkably recovered Germany. Least of all was the VW's significance recognized by the British. Wolfsburg, the home of the ruined VW factory, was in the British Zone, and the British were offered the plant and production rights as reparations. A team of automotive experts was sent from England to evaluate the vehicle and its potential in the marketplace. They concluded that Hitler's "Strength through Joy car," upon which thousands of German families had placed deposits in

the 1930s, could "never be more than a novelty."
Was there a greater mistake in England's history? By
1960, the Beetle had chased every British car in its
class off the American and European markets and
was fueling what the Germans called their
Wirtschaftswunder, their economic miracle. The
experts' mistake is perhaps understandable in light of
the fact that the Wolfsburg plant had never produced
a Beetle, except for a handful of pilot models, before
it was turned over to the production of military
Volkswagens.

But, of course, all of us, seeing a Volkswagen
for the first time, thought it peculiar, to say the least.
That strange-looking body with the droopy snout, the
horribly noisy engine in the back, the lack of a
radiator, all four gears needing double-clutching.
Then there were seats that looked as though they
were covered in GI blankets.

I must have been among the first people to
drive a Beetle, one of the earliest to come off the
assembly line in 1946, and I still remember the
occasion vividly. It came about in an odd way.

The retired colonel in charge of the British
MilGov unit had committed suicide, shooting
himself with a double-barreled shotgun after his
marriage proposal to a young army driver was
rejected. I was called in to certify the suicide, a task
made easy by his having left two notes to explain his
action. The colonel was replaced by a still-serving

major with whom I quickly developed a comfortable relationship, so much so that he proposed that we exchange cars for a few days. He had to go to Frankfurt to a conference and was reluctant to take the long trip in the Volkswagen that had just been issued him. (Nearly all the first Beetles went to the British Army.) He had earlier admired the Horch I was then driving, a large gas guzzler that the German police couldn't possibly afford to run. I had had the car but a couple of weeks, but I agreed to the trade, liking the major as much as I did. He went off the Autobahn somewhere in central Germany, breaking both his legs and wrecking the car. I never saw him or the car again.

The Beetle he left me with, like all the initial models that came off the assembly line, was, in a word, crude. But it was oddly fascinating. My American colleagues were eager to have rides, and I trundled it around Bremerhaven for a while with them until, when I turned a corner sharply, the battery slid from its mooring and the Beetle stopped cold. My colleagues and I were rescued by the MPs, and the British took the VW back. An informant subsequently put me onto an Opel Kadett that I could acquire for many cartons of cigarettes, and it became, shock absorber-less and all, my last German car.

Whenever I ride in my daughter's New Beetle, with its quiet, up-front engine, its automatic transmission, its heated seats, and all the comforts of home, I inevitably recall that first Beetle and think of the worlds that the Old and the New Beetles represent. Does anybody these days stop to recall the "Strength through Joy" idea that Hitler intended the VW to epitomize? Does anybody consider what *Volkswagen* means? Perhaps you had to be there.

CHAPTER TWENTY-FOUR

"Bresnehaven"

In the late spring of 1947, a new commanding general came to Bremerhaven, and a different kind of new day dawned. His name was Bresnehan, and he so quickly and powerfully made his presence felt that GIs soon took to calling the city "Bresnehaven." He was a stickler. He would salute a soldier on the street, steps away from him still, before the enlisted man could salute him, forcing a responsive salute. The GIs were quick to catch on, and there was a lot more enthusiastic saluting of all officers than there had been. The general soon denounced the widespread practice of painting names -- sometimes silly ones, often useful designations -- under the windows of jeeps and trucks. Those vehicles, his declaration told us, were the Army's, and those who had painted the names were guilty of "defacing government property." The names vanished overnight. On the same grounds he made jeep drivers remove the weather-proof tops that had made the vehicles much more pleasant to use. We wondered what was coming next.

We soon found out. The agent in charge returned from a meeting of unit commanders, telling us that he had been ordered to put on his captain's bars. The general thought him "out of uniform" without them. He had been told by an aide to the general that Bresnehan intended to "tame" the CIC. That could only mean, in our imagining, that the general intended to end CIC's privileged status and draw the unit into the Army's embrace. Loud voices insisted that that would be the end of CIC's effectiveness.

At that point it wasn't clear to the agent in charge or anybody else whether Bresnehan was acting alone or in accordance with a general move from the top to reshape CIC everywhere. Did Bresnehan have the authority arbitrarily to "tame" the unit under his command, we wondered? Was he simply following instructions? Such questions hung in the air without anything happening to reveal his intention. Weeks passed without any further change, though we passed on to one another every little Bresnehan anecdote we picked up, looking for clues in them. The captain wore his brass bars, and we continued to call him by his first name and not to salute him.

But there came the day the agents had feared. As of a certain date, all CIC personnel were to wear rank insignia. Morale dropped into the basement. No more evenings of companionable drinking in the officers club! No more purchases of officers' tunics and loafers in the commissary! An end to privilege! It seemed inevitable as the summer moved into the Days of the Dog that the house would be the next to go and with it an end to all those wonderful meals. But that did not happen before I left the unit, by which time we had several new agents who had never known a Counter Intelligence Corps without rank insignia. One of them, a native German speaker who had transferred from an infantry regiment, came to us sporting three stripes and four or five rockers.

Even as we Brits had been directed in the beginning to emulate the practices of our new colleagues in most particulars, so we were now told that we should join the American agents in wearing rank insignia. Accordingly I pinned my brass crowns on the sleeves of my jacket's forearms, with the unhappy sense that I, too, had been "tamed" and was being returned to an army I had had little to do with for so many months.

By that time I was finding very little interesting work to do. It had become a rare thing for me to have a case sent up from Bremen, just as rare for me to get a mail intercept to investigate. I continued to meet with my informants, but the time I spent with them was less like intelligence work than it was socializing. I found myself pleased to be asked to interview a potential war bride, a change from an increasingly dull routine.

But in my private life there was a huge change. Sergeant Shelley and I were married in accordance with German law, which is to say that we were married by the *Bürgermeister* of Bremerhaven -- in German, of course. To reach that happy point, we had both had to seek the permission of our superiors. In my case, getting married required only that I drive to Hamburg and obtain an Army license, with no change in my official status. In Gretchen's case, however, it meant traveling to Frankfurt by train, there to be honorably discharged from the Army, for in those days a married woman could not be a WAC.

We had a weekend honeymoon in the village of Brake, on the other side of the Weser, in the home of an American couple who had befriended us. Afterwards, I returned to my room in the CIC house, where women were not allowed above the ground floor, while Gretchen, now a civilian, returned to the Dependents' Hotel. We were told that there was no housing available for which we could qualify, since we had no children, and it seemed as though we should have to live apart until I had served out my time.

But one day, driving through the *Bürgerpark* area for some reason, I noticed that there was a tiny house beyond a large expanse of vegetable garden where an elderly German was tying plants to stakes. On impulse, I stepped out of my car and walked over to him. He told me that he had been given permission to grow vegetables (which he was doing splendidly) by the woman who was living in the little house. She, he told me directly, was German and the girlfriend of an American officer. Hmm! Surely we would have a greater claim on the house than somebody's mistress.

Without telling Gretchen about my discovery, I went to see the officer in charge of housing assignments. Happily, he was a man with whom I had dealt pleasantly on an earlier occasion. He was at once sympathetic, and I quickly gathered that he had been more than a little irritated that the German woman was living in an area of the city that was otherwise entirely American. Neither did he approve of fellow officers sleeping with the enemy.

I have no idea what strings he had to pull or what he had to say to his colleague to cause the woman to leave, but leave she did within a few days, and we moved in. The place was little more than a cabin, but it had plumbing and heating, a bathroom and a kitchen, a place where we could live comfortably, while we continued to take most of our meals at the CIC house.

I chatted with the constant gardener from time to time, always impressed by the remarkable orderliness of his beds and the growing evidence of his success in rows of green beans, cabbages, and the like. Being no gardener myself, there were things flourishing there that I didn't recognize. I found out one day, though, that one of the unknowns was corn, when an American woman knocked at the door and, after greeting me with a smile of delight and some puzzlement about my identity, explained that she had just helped herself to a dozen ears of corn. Seeing them as she drove by, she "just couldn't resist taking a few." She was most eager to pay for what she had taken and was surprised to find me in the house, rather than the German gardener she had expected. How could she pay for what she had taken, she asked me. I suggested that she bring me a carton of cigarettes and I would give it to the gardener when next I saw him. She was most happy with what seemed to her a real bargain. She was bubbling at the thought of her husband's delight when she told him they were going to have fresh corn on the cob for dinner. The next day she was back with a carton and a while later I presented it to the gardener. He was overwhelmed by my explanation of the settlement, having assumed that I had taken the corn and didn't intend to pay him. All along, his plan had been to find American buyers, although he had never imagined that he could get that kind of price. I served for a few weeks as his agent in other sales, making him comfortable in the process. Somehow, it pleased me to see a decent economic exchange going on between the two sides.

My replacement had arrived earlier, a Canadian civilian in the employ of the British Military Government. He had earned a master's degree in German studies at the University of Toronto, so his

German was fluent, and he had an extensive knowledge of German history and literature. He was to work with me for the few weeks until my departure, and we quickly became friends. I often wished that I had had his kind of education and training before I entered Germany.

Word came shortly before I left that the CIC house was to be closed down; the three apartments would become homes for three American families. Two of the CIC's commissioned officers were already living elsewhere with their families; the third, a bachelor, would find a place in the officers' quarters on *Hafenstrasse*. The enlisted men would move to barracks and mess hall. What a comedown! The unit's morale was completely destroyed. Mercifully, those drastic changes did not come to pass while I was still part of the unit, and to the day of our departure for England the wonderful meals were still flowing from Charlie's kitchen.

It was an emotional leave-taking for me, a parting from close friends whose languages, American and German, I had increasingly made my own. But I left with the certain knowledge that, while I had come two years before to Bremerhaven, it was "Bresnehaven" I was leaving behind.

ABOUT THE AUTHOR

Bruce Haywood served as provost of Kenyon College in Gambier, Ohio for seventeen years, and as president of Monmouth College in the Illinois town of that name for fourteen years. Born in 1925 in Yorkshire, England, he served with British Army Intelligence in Germany at the conclusion of World War II, then continued his education at Leeds University. He earned his baccalaureate at McGill University and, in 1956, his doctorate at Harvard University.

His previous books include *Novalis: The Veil of Imagery, A Study of the Poetic Works of Friedrich Von Hardenberg (1772-1801)*, published in 1959 by Harvard University Press; *The Essential College*, published in 2006 by XOXOX Press; and *Allerton Bywater*, published in the following year under the same imprint.

Gretchen Shelley Haywood passed away in 2003. The author subsequently married Mary Bailey. The couple resides in Galesburg, Illinois.

The author in 1946 ...

Ted Rice

... and today

92 Intelligence Team, Late Spring, 1947. By this time, only three members of the original team remained: John Garrett (far left), the author (fourth from left), and Captain Draycott (center).

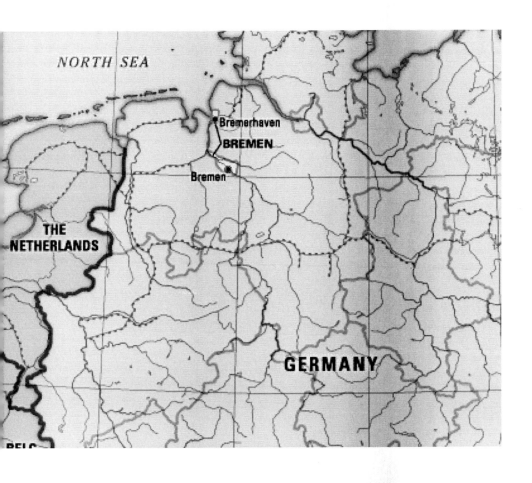

This map shows the location of Land
Bremen, a federal state, within modern
Germany. Its area approximates that of
the Bremen Enclave.